SMART START GARDEN PLANNER

Your Step-by-Step Guide to a Successful Season

MEGAN CAIN

The Creative Vegetable Gardener

For Mark.
My favorite partner in all of life's colorful
adventures, inside the garden and out.

Smart Start Garden Planner: Your Step-by-Step Guide
 to a Successful Season

ISBN 978-0-692-83210-3
First Edition
Published by Megan Cain,
The Creative Vegetable Gardener - Madison, WI

Author: Megan Cain
Photos: Megan Cain, Mark Sundlin,
Nick Wilkes Photography
Design: Rebecca Pollock

CreativeVegetableGardener.com

Is this book for you?

Our community of gardeners is big and colorful, and it spans the entire globe. Some of us are planting avocado trees and picking limes for dinner in our own little tropical paradise, some of us have gardens that are covered in a deep layer of snow all winter long, and some of us are tending to our container gardens up on the 15th floor of a high rise.

We're an eclectic bunch!

But one thing that many of us have in common is that we care about getting results for our gardening efforts. We're not interested in bumbling our way through the process, wasting money and time as we go.

This sounds like you, doesn't it?

You love the idea of having a successful garden that feeds healthy food to you and your family. But you're incredibly busy with work, school, kids, family, cooking, and household chores and don't have endless hours to devote to gardening.

You're in the right place. This book will guide you through creating a clear plan for the upcoming gardening season that will help you get more from your garden, sooner. You'll skip over the common beginner mistakes and feel confident, prepared, and excited about your garden.

Garden planning may sound like a big task, but we're going to keep it practical, down-to-earth, and fun! You're not going to do anything that's too complicated or takes too much time. We're in it for the least amount of work possible that delivers the best results.
I'm going to walk you through each step, and at the end of the workbook you'll have a personalized blueprint for what a successful season in your garden will look like.

If you're the kind of gardener who wants to give the gardening lifestyle a real try, honing and developing your skills so that you get the most from your garden, year after year, this book is for you.

Welcome!

Contents

What is a smart garden?

It's a beautiful garden that yields lots of food for the least amount of time and money invested.

Does this sound impossible? Believe me, it's not.

Gardening is a lot of work—joyful work for sure—and I've met lots of gardeners over the years who aren't getting the most from their gardens. And if you're not seeing real results, well . . . gardening isn't as rewarding a pastime as it should be.

Your garden should add to your life by bringing you more of the things that breathe color into your days—things like food, beauty, health, pleasure, and joy. Not more of the things that bring you stress, like weeds, pests, and failing vegetable plants.

A smart garden is all about more of the former and way less of the latter.

So, how do you go about creating a smart garden? By transforming yourself into a smart gardener.

And what's the first thing a smart gardener does? She plans her garden. The most successful gardeners I know take some time before the garden season begins to devise a simple plan for the year.

Smart garden planning is more than figuring out how much space you have or deciding where you're going to purchase your seeds and plants. It's a more holistic way of thinking about how you want to approach your garden each season.

In the following pages, you'll learn how to take a step back and look at this bigger picture by examining your weekly eating and shopping habits, imagining the pleasures you want your garden to bring to your life this year, and learning to look at each vegetable with a strategic eye.

So, cozy up in your favorite chair with a steaming hot cup of your favorite drink (hot chocolate with marshmallows? Black coffee? Tea made from dried herbs from your garden?) and immerse yourself in your hopes and dreams for this year's garden.

They really can come true. You just need to make a plan for them!

Megan

DESIGN YOUR SMART GARDEN

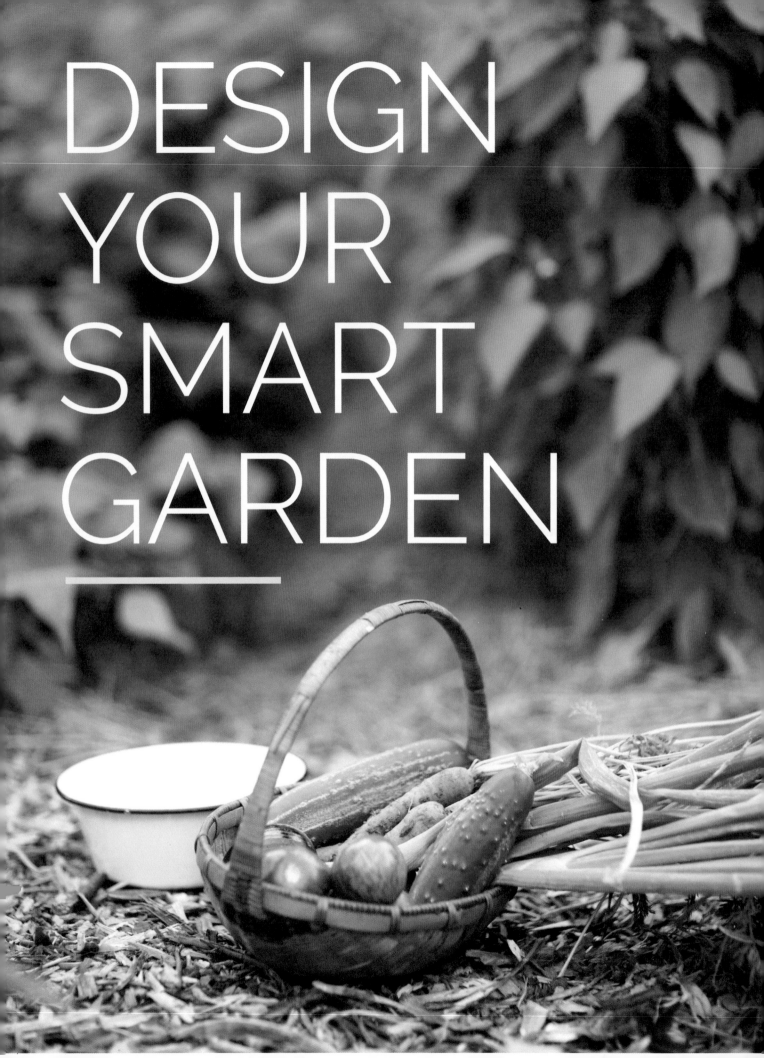

As gardeners, we're all dreamers, right?

We take a miniscule seed from a colorful packet and gently place it in the soil. And in that seed is the dream of what's to come—a bright yellow carrot, a huge tomato plant, or a sprawling squash vine.

Anything is possible in a life filled with a garden!

This beginning stage of the garden-planning process is the perfect time to think more deeply about the role you want your garden to play in your life; our gardens can be about so much more than just growing food for our tables if we let them.

Garden Reflection

Before you jump in and start planning for next season, take a few minutes to reflect on the past one.

Grab a cup of warm tea and relax in your favorite chair. Close your eyes and transport yourself into last year's garden. Travel through the months and recall the many sights, sounds, and smells of each season of your garden.

If you had a year with more failures than successes, or you were too overwhelmed to even start your garden and are disappointed with yourself, release last year's garden (and the gardener you were!) with kindness and love. The beautiful thing about gardening is that it's a cyclical journey. The slate is wiped clean each winter, and we begin anew each spring.

Then, take a moment to read each question on the **Garden Reflection** worksheet and jot down some notes. You're starting to lay the strong foundation for the new garden season by deciding what you'd like to repeat and what you'd like to leave behind.

Remember that each season holds successes and failures, even for the most experienced gardener. There's a certain amount of mystery to gardening, which is one of the things that makes it so exciting. But it can also be frustrating and disappointing when things don't work out as planned.

During your reflection remind yourself that there is no such thing as a perfect garden. Every garden is a work in progress. Part of the fun is the journey, so don't forget to embrace and celebrate every part of it.

You can print out a copy of this worksheet at creativevegetablegardener.com/ smart-planning-book.

GARDEN REFLECTION

Describe last year's garden in a few words.

What were my successes last year?

What did I struggle with?

What do I wish I had done differently and/or better last year?

When I think about the coming year, is there anything that I'm worried about?

What do I want to learn more about this coming year?

I grew too much of this in my garden:

I wish I had more of this in my garden:

Other thoughts or reflections:

Your Garden and Life Vision for This Year

Now that you've spent some time looking back, let's turn our attention to the upcoming season. But before we talk specifically about your particular garden, I want you to zoom out and think about the bigger picture.

When you immerse yourself in gardening it becomes more than a hobby . . . it becomes a lifestyle. It starts with trying to grow food and eventually ends up adding color to your entire life—the way you think about food, how you cook dinner for your family, the way you look at the world.

So, let's think big!

What kind of lifestyle do you want gardening to create for you this year?

Maybe you want to spend more time just relaxing in your favorite chair in your garden, or learning photography so you can take better pictures of your harvest. Perhaps you want to get more exercise by taking a walk in your neighborhood each evening after you water your plants, or you want to try one new healthy recipe a week throughout harvest season.

Let gardening be the theme that is woven through everything and allow it to bring more meaning to your life this year. Use the following worksheet to spend a few minutes reflecting on and journaling about this question.

MY GARDEN VISION FOR THIS YEAR

Circle all of the things you'd like more of in your life:

Photography	Relaxation	Working on creative/artistic projects
More physical activity	More visual beauty	
Honing your cooking skills	More time with family	
Appreciating nature	A focused hobby	
Being outside more	Eating right	
Learning about plants	Entertaining at home	

Pick your top three from the list above and write a few sentences about how you'll use them and your garden to pursue your ideal lifestyle.

What kind of lifestyle do I want gardening to create for me this year?

Next, I want you to create a Pinterest board that represents the kind of lifestyle you want gardening to create for you this year.

As gardeners, we tend to be visual people who think in images, colors, and patterns. Using a platform like Pinterest is a way to stimulate your creativity and get your brain excited to start the planning process. It's like an electronic version of a vision board. It's a way to state your intentions for the season, and it's something tangible you can return to throughout the year to rekindle that vision when you need a reminder.

Take the themes that arose when you answered the questions on the worksheet and search for photos that represent them visually. You can check out my board, My Garden Visions and Goals, as inspiration here: pinterest.com/createveggies/my-garden-visions-goals/.

If Pinterest isn't your thing, create your vision board in another medium. You might draw pictures or assemble a collage with cuttings from magazines and seed catalogs. When you've created your board, come share it in the free Facebook group I run for gardeners all over the world - Creative Gardener Challenges. You can request to join here: facebook.com/groups/MakeYourHarvestLast/. We'd love to be inspired by your ideas and support you in accomplishing your vision this year.

What Do You Want to Grow?

One of the most fun parts of the garden-planning process is thinking about what you want to grow in your garden this year. Most of us don't have enough room to grow everything we'd like, unless we have a mini-farm! Spend some time strategizing so you can get the most from your garden this season.

Instead of running out to the nursery on the first nice day of spring and throwing plants and seeds into your cart willy-nilly (I've been there!), be more deliberate in your choices this year. Before deciding what to grow, use the following questions to take a closer look at your family's eating habits and what you buy at the grocery store on a regular basis.

WHAT DO I WANT TO GROW?

What does my family eat and buy from the grocery store on a regular basis?

Which of these ingredients can I grow for myself?

What is most important for me to have fresh from my garden?

What foods taste noticeably better when I grow them myself? (If you don't know, which foods do you enjoy more from the farmers market as opposed to the grocery store?)

What special varieties do I want that are hard to find?

Which foods provide the highest value? What's expensive to buy or difficult to find in winter? (Examples: berries, red peppers, broccoli)

Are there foods that I want to preserve for winter eating? If so, what can I easily preserve? (Examples: tomato sauce, pesto, garlic)

What's grown well for me in the past? What have I seen growing well in my neighborhood, or received as excess from friends or coworkers?

What will make me happy to grow in my garden?

Next, use your answers to the questions on the previous worksheet to help you choose what vegetables you want to grow in your garden with the My Vegetable List worksheet.

To get the most bang for your buck, consider prioritizing the vegetables that showed up in your answers.

For example, my answer to question two—*What is most important to me to have fresh from my garden?*—is spinach, herbs, red peppers, and kale. Why? Because I love to eat a spinach salad most nights with dinner and I also use spinach as a main ingredient in my morning smoothie. Herbs are expensive at the grocery store and they spoil quickly, so being able to run out to my garden and snip a few for a recipe saves me so much money throughout the season.

Fresh red peppers are like gold to me! I love having more than we can eat during the summer so I can share them with friends and neighbors. They always feel like such a valuable gift to give! In summer, when it's too hot to grow spinach in my garden, I use massaged kale salads to replace my nightly spinach salad.

Like my answers, think about what you like to eat and the lifestyle you're trying to create when you fill out the worksheet.

Use the checkboxes on the following worksheet to choose what you'd like to grow this season. There are some extra columns if you want to mark down how much you eat per week or if you already know how many plants or feet of the vegetable you want in your garden. If not, don't worry about that right now.

This is just your first draft. Later in the book we'll be talking about how to narrow down your list. Have fun!

MY VEGETABLE LIST

✔	Vegetable	I eat this much per week	I'd like this many plants or feet of this vegetable	Notes (varieties you like, whether you'd like some extra for canning, freezing or giving away)
	Arugula			
	Asparagus			*Perennial. Grows best in a separate bed.*
	Beans, Fresh			
	Beans, Dry			
	Beets			
	Bok Choy			
	Broccoli			
	Brussels Sprouts			
	Cabbage			
	Carrots			
	Cauliflower			
	Celery			
	Collards			
	Corn			
	Cucumbers			
	Edamame (Soybeans)			
	Eggplant			
	Fennel			
	Garlic			
	Kale			
	Kohlrabi			
	Leeks			
	Lettuce, Head			
	Lettuce, Salad Mix			
	Melons			

✔	Vegetable	I eat this much per week	I'd like this many plants or feet of this vegetable	Notes (varieties you like, whether you'd like some extra for canning, freezing or giving away)
	Okra			
	Onions			
	Parsnips			
	Peas			
	Peppers, Sweet			
	Peppers, Hot			
	Potatoes			
	Pumpkins			
	Radishes			
	Raspberries			*Perennial. Grows best in a separate bed.*
	Rhubarb			*Perennial. Grows best in a separate bed.*
	Scallions			
	Shallots			
	Spinach			
	Squash, Summer			
	Squash, Winter			
	Strawberries			*Perennial. Grows best in a separate bed.*
	Sweet Potaotes			
	Swiss Chard			
	Tomatillos			
	Tomatoes, Cherry			
	Tomatoes, Roma			
	Tomatoes, Slicing			
	Turnips			
	Other			
	Other			

HERBS

✔	Herb	Number of plants desired	Notes (varieties you like, whether you'd like some extra for canning, freezing or giving away)
	Basil		*Annual in cold climates*
	Cilantro CORIANDR		*Annual in cold climates*
	Dill		*Annual in cold climates, but re-seeds itself*
	Garlic Chives		*Perennial*
	Marjoram		*Perennial*
	Mint		*Perennial*
	Onion Chives		*Perennial*
	Oregano		*Perennial*
	Parsley KECRLÍK		*Annual in cold climates*
	Rosemary		*Perennial, but won't survive winter in cold areas*
	Sage		*Perennial*
	Tarragon /ESTRKGON PELYNĚK		*Perennial*
	Thyme		*Perennial*
	Other		

FLOWERS

✔	Flower	Number of plants desired	Notes
	Rudbeckia		
	Sunflowers		
	Sweet Peas		
	Verbena Bonariensis		
	Zinnias		
	Other		
	Other		
	Other		
	Other		

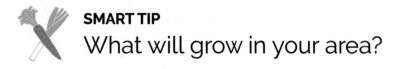

SMART TIP
What will grow in your area?

It's wonderful to imagine millions of us gardeners tending to our own plots of land all over the world! But the truth of world-wide gardening means living in very different climates and zones.

The vegetables listed in the **My Vegetable List** worksheet are the most commonly grown vegetables.

If you live in a very high-altitude location, or the tropics, or a desert, you many need to do some additional research to find out what plants thrive in your location.

The best way to do your research? Talk to other gardeners in your city or town and find out what grows best for them. You could also make some visits to your local farmers' market and observe what the farmers in your area are growing in their fields. Your state university's cooperative extension office may have free articles and publications about growing vegetables in your home state. Here's an example of Wisconsin's website: https://learningstore.uwex.edu/

However you do it, finding out what grows where you live will make your smart garden that much more successful—you'll be working with the environment rather than against it.

It's Time to Order Your Seed Catalogs

If you don't currently receive seed catalogs at home, you're really missing out!

It's so fun to peek inside your mailbox on a cold and dreary winter day and find a colorful seed catalog poking out. One of my favorite weekend activities in winter is to curl up next to my wood stove with a stack of catalogs and gardening books and let my imagination wander. The most successful gardeners I know order their seeds ahead of time and are ready to go when the season starts.

By the end of this workbook, you'll be ready to put in your own seed order. But first, you'll need to request some catalogs in the mail. (If you don't like to receive paper in the mail, you can shop online on each of these companies' websites.)

They take a few weeks to arrive, so I recommend going to your computer right now and putting in your requests. Here are some of my favorites to get you started. To keep things simple, I don't recommend ordering more than three catalogs to start.

U.S. GARDENERS:

- **Johnny's Selected Seeds** – used by lots of professional CSA farmers johnnyseeds.com
- **Seed Savers Exchange** – non-profit in Iowa that sells only heirloom varieties seedsavers.org
- **High Mowing Seeds** – all of the seeds they sell are organic highmowingseeds.com
- **Hudson Valley Seed Library** – small company in upstate NY that hires artists to create art for their seed packets seedlibrary.org

CANADIAN GARDENERS:

- **Urban Harvest** – organic and heirloom seeds uharvest.ca
- **Sow True Seed** – organic, heirloom and traditional varieties sowtrueseed.com

It'll take a week or so to get your catalogs in the mail. In the meantime you can work your way through the rest of this workbook and we'll revisit the catalogs again later.

VEGGIE ESSENTIALS

Getting to Know the Different Characteristics of Vegetables

A few years ago my sister called me from Philadelphia, where she was learning to garden, and asked me,

"When you plant one onion, how many onions do you get?"

Wow! This one question completely reframed things for me. I had never quite thought about each vegetable in this way. And when I told her that she would get one onion from planting one onion, she said, *"Oh, then I'm not going to plant them. It won't be worth it."*

When you start to examine the garden in this light, there are clearly things that are more "worth it" to grow than others.

When you plant a vegetable like tomatoes, you obviously get a lot of bang for your buck. You plant one seedling, wait three months, and then get to harvest pounds and pounds of tomatoes just from that one plant. That's a pretty good investment for a $3 seedling. On the other hand, when you plant a cabbage seedling, you wait about 70 days and then harvest one cabbage. That's it, no more, it's over. If you want to get anything more out of that space, you'll have to rip out the remaining cabbage carcass and plant something else.

Hmmm, which one sounds like a better investment to you? Well, it might depend on how much you love cabbage and hate tomatoes. Maybe you eat sauerkraut every day for lunch, so you can't wait to fill your garden with it. The answer all depends on your perspective.

It's important to know a bit more about the different categories of vegetable so you can make a strategic decision based on your priorities, your garden size, and what the people in your house like to eat.

In What Season Will You Get the Harvest?

In most climates, we associate various foods with different times of the year.

The changing seasons bring summer picnics with watermelon juice dripping down our chins, fall dinners with steaming hot butternut squash soup, and winter holiday gatherings featuring Brussels sprouts and potato dishes.

The reason different foods are tied to the seasons is that vegetables grow best at certain times of the year. Knowing in which season you can expect the harvest will help you plan a garden that produces beautiful food for your table for as many months of the season as possible.

⟹ GET MORE BANG FOR THE BUCK = PŘIJÍT SI NA SVÉ ZA
VYDANÉ PENÍZE; NEPROHLOUPIT; ROZUMNĚ
UTRATIT S CO NEJVĚTŠÍM UŽITKEM

SPRING

One common mistake I see many vegetable gardeners make is waiting until after their last frost in spring to begin planting their gardens. This is a mistake because there are many vegetables that prefer, and even thrive, in the cooler temperatures of spring. They are frost hardy and can easily survive when temperatures hover around freezing.

Some of them do not like the hot weather of summer and won't grow well at that time of year. You'll likely need to take a break planting these vegetables in the middle of summer. For example, arugula and cilantro will start to shoot up flowers (called bolting) when they get stressed from the heat.

Other plants are less picky and can survive the hot days and nights of summer just fine. Kale loves the spring weather, but continues to grow and produce harvests during the dog days of summer as well.

Spring-harvested vegetables:

arugula, asparagus, beets, bok choy, broccoli, cabbage, cauliflower, cilantro, collards, fennel, kale, kohlrabi, lettuce (head), marjoram, mint, onion chives, oregano, parsley, peas, radishes, rhubarb, sage, salad mix, scallions, spinach, swiss chard, tarragon, turnips, thyme

What does this mean for garden planning?

Often the early harvests of the season are the ones we're most excited about after a long winter. Plant these vegetables as early as possible so you can reap the rewards in spring. If you wait until after your last frost, you won't be harvesting them until summer.

SUMMER

Many of the summer vegetables are planted after the danger of frost has passed in your area. They don't like the cool weather of spring and often can't survive if the temperatures dip below freezing. Once the weather in your garden warms up and starts feeling like summer, you'll notice these plants starting to grow more quickly. They love the heat!

Some of the spring vegetables from the previous list are repeated here because they're less picky about the temperatures in which they grow. Beets can be planted in early spring a month before your last frost, but they can also be replanted throughout the summer since they don't mind the heat. Most of the perennial herbs come up in spring and can be harvested throughout the entire season.

Summer-harvested vegetables:

basil, beans, beets, cabbage, carrots, celery, collards, corn, cucumbers, dill, edamame, eggplant, garlic, garlic chives, kale, marjoram, melons, mint, okra, onions, onion chives, oregano, parsley, rosemary, peppers, potatoes, raspberries, sage, scallions, shallots, summer squash, strawberries, swiss chard, tarragon, thyme, tomatillos, tomatoes

What does this mean for garden planning?

Some of these vegetables, like carrots, are planted in spring, but because they take so long to grow they're not ready to harvest until the summer. Make sure you pick at least a few vegetables from this list for those luscious summer harvests.

FALL

Fall is often the peak of harvest time in the vegetable garden. Summer vegetables like tomatoes and eggplant are still producing and are joined by fall vegetables like winter squash and Brussels sprouts.

You can also replant some of quicker-growing spring vegetables for a fall garden. As fall approaches, the hot-weather crops start to slow down, but the cool-weather vegetables like spinach and lettuce really start to thrive!

Some of the vegetables producing a harvest in the fall are not frost tolerant. This means vegetables like tomatoes and peppers will die as soon as the temperatures dip below 32 degrees F. But the cool-weather vegetables like broccoli and Brussels sprouts will often live many weeks into the fall and early winter even as the temperatures get down into the twenties and teens F.

Fall-harvested vegetables:

arugula, basil, beans, beets, bok choy, broccoli, brussels sprouts, cabbage, carrots, cauliflower, celery, cilantro, collards, corn, cucumbers, dill, edamame, eggplant, garlic chives, kale, kohlrabi, leeks, lettuce (head), marjoram, melons, mint, okra, onion chives, oregano, parsley, parsnips, peppers, potatoes, pumpkins, radishes, raspberries, rosemary, sage, salad mix, scallions, shallots, spinach, summer squash, sweet potatoes, swiss chard, tarragon, thyme, tomatillos, tomatoes, turnips, winter squash

What does this mean for garden planning?

If there are spring vegetables you love, consider planting a fall crop of them. I always plant several beds of spinach in late summer, and they provide me with many dinner salads throughout the fall and early winter. The trick to having a fall garden is to start thinking about it in summer, when most of the planting needs to happen.

WINTER

Depending on what kind of climate you live and garden in, you may be able to harvest some vegetables throughout the winter. Even in Wisconsin, where I live in zone 5a, I harvest from my garden until Thanksgiving and sometimes even Christmas, depending on the weather.

These vegetables are the most cold hardy and can survive temperatures down into the teens and twenties F. But, with the exception of spinach and the perennial herbs, most of the vegetables will eventually die if you live in a climate where it gets down into single digits and below zero F.

Winter-harvested vegetables:

beets, brussels sprouts, carrots, collards, garlic chives, kale, leeks, marjoram, mint, onion chives, oregano, parsnips, sage, scallions, spinach, tarragon, thyme, turnips

What does this mean for garden planning?

Knowing you can harvest some of these vegetables in all four seasons of the year may convince you to grow them in your garden this season. They give you a pretty good bang for your buck!

Dig In:

Now it's time to take a look at the vegetables you chose on the **My Vegetable List** worksheet and familiarize yourself with the time of year when they're harvested. Use the first column of the **Veggie Essentials Cheat Sheet** at the end of the book to review each vegetable and make sure your list contains vegetables from spring, summer, and fall.

How Much Food Will You Harvest From Each Plant?

The different vegetables you'll plant in your garden produce widely different amounts of food. Ever hear of National Sneak a Zucchini Onto Your Neighbor's Porch Day? Yes, it's a thing! And it gives you a clue about how much food a zucchini plant might produce. The answer is a lot!

That's why it's important to understand how much food you'll get from each plant throughout the season when deciding whether you want to grow it in your garden. If you don't really like zucchini you might want to skip planting it in your garden and replace it with something else instead!

PLANT ONE – Harvest One

In this category are vegetables that produce one thing to harvest for each seed or seedling you plant. When the seed or seedling matures, you'll harvest the whole thing and it won't re-grow.

Let's go back to my sister's question. *How many onions do you get when you plant an onion?* The answer is one. One onion seedling equals one onion.

Broccoli is another example. When you plant one broccoli plant it will produce one large head of broccoli after about 65 days. You'll harvest that head and it won't grow another one. It may continue to put out little baby broccolis (called side shoots), but you'll never get another big one on the same plant.

These vegetables produce one vegetable for each seed or seedling you plant in the garden:

beets, bok choy, broccoli, cabbage, carrots, cauliflower, celery, fennel, garlic, kohlrabi, leeks, lettuce (head), onions, parsnips, radishes, scallions, shallots, turnips

What does this mean for garden planning?

Think about each vegetable in this category and decide whether you want to devote the space and time to it. Often, but not always, these vegetables ripen all at once, so you'll need to deal with the whole crop in a short window of time. If you plant 12 broccoli plants of the same variety on the same day in April, they'll all be ready for harvest at about the same time. But a bonus for vegetables that get harvested all at once is that you often have time to plant something else in their place. I usually plant my fall carrots and beets in the space from which I harvest my onions in July.

Some of these vegetables are great candidates for succession planting. You can replant them several times throughout the season for a continued harvest.

PLANT ONE – Harvest for a Short Time

The vegetables in this category all provide a few harvests and then they stop producing for different reasons (heat, time of the season, end of plant life).

If you've ever grown cilantro in your garden, you've probably noticed that once it grows to harvest size you'll get the chance to go out on a few different occasions and harvest some cilantro for dinner. But eventually the plants start flowering and then go to seed, and you can't harvest from them anymore. This is a perfect illustration of how the vegetables in this category work.

Bush beans are another example. When you plant a row of seeds, each one will grow into a plant. And each plant produces more than one bean. Once they're ready for harvest, you can go back to the plants every few days to pick a bowl for supper. But after a few weeks, the beans will slow down and eventually stop producing because they're at the end of their natural life cycle. You'll need to plant a new row if you want green beans again that season. Unlike the last category where each vegetable produced one item per seed or seedling, vegetables in this category do produce more than one vegetable per seed, but the harvest doesn't go on indefinitely.

These vegetables produce more than one veggie for each seed or seedling you plant, but only for a finite amount of time:

arugula, asparagus, bush beans, brussels sprouts, cilantro, corn, dill, edamame, melons, peas, potatoes, pumpkins, raspberries, rhubarb, salad mix, spinach, strawberries, sweet potatoes, winter squash

What does this mean for garden planning?

If you want a continued supply of your favorites from this category, some of them can be planted multiple times throughout the season (succession planting).

Keep in mind that many of the plants will remain in their garden spaces for much of the season, even though they may only produce for a limited amount of time. For example, winter squash takes over 110 days to produce fruit.

Because you often have only a short time to deal with the harvest, be careful of how much you plant if you don't think you'll be able to eat it all or preserve it when it's ready. (I'm looking at you, bush beans!)

PLANT ONE - Harvest for a Long Time

These plants are a great bang for their buck! Once they get to harvest stage, they'll produce food for many weeks or months as they continue to grow new leaves and fruit throughout the season.

For example, a basil seedling planted in early summer will produce for many months. The leaves and plant will continue to grow, so you'll be able to go back to the same plant for many dinner harvests. Basil will often keep producing right up until your first frost in fall. Kale is another great example. After you plant a kale seedling you'll be harvesting from the plant for the rest of the season, even weeks after your first frost!

These vegetables produce food for many weeks or months of the season once they get to harvest size:

basil, celery, fall cilantro, collards, cucumbers, eggplant, kale, mint, okra, parsley, peppers, pole beans, fall/winter spinach, summer squash, swiss chard, tomatillos, tomatoes, perennial herbs like sage, oregano, thyme, mint, etc.

What does this mean for garden planning?

You could choose to plant more of these vegetables because they produce a continued supply of food in your garden. You'll also have an extended period of time to deal with the harvest since it doesn't come all at once.

Remember that they'll remain in place for most of the garden season, so you won't be able to plant anything else in that space. Also, make sure you really like to eat these vegetables or you might get sick of them after a while! I pulled out my okra plants one year even though they were still producing because I just couldn't eat them anymore.

Dig In:

Take a look at the vegetables you selected on the **My Vegetable List** worksheet and see which category they fall into. Knowing whether they produce once, for a short period of time, or for the whole season should help you evaluate whether you think they're worth it to grow in your garden this season.

The point of this part of the planning process is for you to pick the vegetables that are perfect for your own eating and cooking preferences. If it doesn't seem worth it to you to grow onions, give yourself permission to leave them off your garden plan this season. Buy them from the farmers' market instead!

You can now evaluate each vegetable using two different characteristics: during which season it grows and how much food it will produce. Use the **Veggie Essentials Cheat Sheet** at the back of the book to help you. Does the combination of these two factors make you look at any of the vegetables you chose differently?

How Big Do the Plants Grow?

Sometimes, when we're holding a seed or small plant, we have trouble imagining how big it will grow. This often means things get planted too close and become overgrown, which effects how well each plant produces.

Or, on the flip side, plants may get planted way too far apart because of a fear of how big they may grow, which can result in a lot of wasted of space. This isn't good either! It's important to understand the mature size of the various vegetables. Knowing how much room they're going to take up in your garden will help you plan how many you want to grow, or maybe influence whether you decide to grow them at all!

SMALL

Small vegetable plants are the shortest crops in the garden, growing to be less than 12 inches tall. Because of their compact size, they can often be placed around and underneath other vegetables. For example, some gardeners will interplant quick-growing lettuces around slower growing broccoli because the broccoli will get so much taller than the lettuce, and the lettuce doesn't mind a little shade.

You can often fit a lot of these vegetables in a small space, which leads to a bigger harvest than you might expect.

Vegetables that remain small:

arugula, basil (some), cilantro, garlic chives (can spread over time), lettuce (head, some), marjoram, mint, onions, oregano (can spread over time), radishes, salad mix, scallions, shallots, spinach, strawberries (short but spreading), thyme (can spread over time)

What does this mean for garden planning?

If you have a small garden, you might think about growing more of these vegetables to increase your harvest in the same space. If you have a medium or large-sized garden then you likely have plenty of room for small vegetables! Make sure you don't plant them on the north side of larger plants or they may end up in the shade, which will stunt their growth.

MEDIUM

Many of the most common vegetables we plant in our gardens fall into the medium-sized category. They stay fairly compact and well-behaved, growing between two and three feet tall. They don't tend to spread, sprawl, or get too large.

You can fit a good amount of these in a garden bed, so you'll want to be mindful of how many you plant to make sure you're not getting too much (or too little if you really love it!). A common vegetable that is often overplanted is bush beans. I often hear from gardeners that they have so many beans they don't know what to do with them.

In contrast, is there any such thing as too many red peppers? Not in my garden. I often plant as many as 40 peppers each season.

Vegetables that grow to medium size:

asparagus, basil, beans (bush), beets, bok choy, broccoli, carrots, cauliflower, celery, collards, edamame, eggplant, fennel, garlic, kale, kohlrabi, leeks, lettuce (head), onion chives, parsley, parsnips, peppers, potatoes, rosemary, sage, swiss chard, turnips

What does this mean for garden planning?

Most of these plants can fit almost any garden situation. If you have a small garden, you may choose to plant less of these. If you have a large garden you might focus on planting more.

LARGE

While these vegetables start out as seeds and small plants, they eventually grow to many times their size. Sometimes it's hard to believe how much they'll grow in the course of a few short months! This is one of the miracles of gardening, I think.

There are several different ways these plants are big. They can be tall like Brussels sprouts and tomatoes, wide like cabbage and summer squash, or sprawling vines like winter squash and pumpkins.

Be careful when growing these vegetables, they need a lot of room to stretch out. They can be bullies, sometimes overtaking and smothering the plants around them.

Vegetables that grow to a large size:

beans (pole), brussels sprouts, cabbage, collards, corn, cucumbers, dill, melons, okra, peas, pumpkins, raspberries, rosemary, rhubarb, summer squash, sweet potatoes, tarragon, tomatillos, tomatoes, winter squash

What does this mean for garden planning?

Be mindful of where you plant these big guys. Consider grouping them in one section of the garden, away from the smaller and medium-sized vegetables. Some of the vining plants can be grown up on a trellis to conserve space.

Dig In:

Take a look at each vegetable you selected on the **My Vegetable List** worksheet and pay attention to which size category they're in. Does this affect whether you want to grow them or not? You can also check the **Spacing Guide** on pg. 103 to get a better idea of how much room they'll take up in your garden.

You can now evaluate each vegetable using three different characteristics: during which season it grows, how much food it will produce, and how big it will grow. Use the **Veggie Essentials Cheat Sheet** at the back of the book to help you. Does the combination of these three factors make you look at any of the vegetables you chose differently?

SMART TIP

How big a plant will get can vary greatly between different gardens.

There are lots of different factors that will affect plant size, such as the amount of sun your garden receives, the health of your soil, which gardening region you live in, and what variety you're growing. This is why it's so important to keep records. Over time you'll learn more about what works in your own garden.

How Many Days Until You Get a Harvest?

To a certain extent, gardening feels like a waiting game. Once we get our plants and seeds into the ground, we immediately start looking forward to the day when we can harvest the food. But vegetables vary widely in the number of days they need to grow until we can harvest them for dinner.

Radishes are ready to eat in as little as 21 days, while Brussels sprouts can take up to 110 days. That's a huge difference! Part of strategically deciding what you want to grow in your garden is knowing the time investment for each vegetable.

QUICK TO HARVEST – Short-Season Vegetables

These vegetables go from seed or seedling to harvest size in 40 days or less, which is pretty quick in garden time! I like to plant as many of these vegetables as possible in early spring when I'm starved for fresh vegetables from the garden. I want a quick harvest!

They're also a fun choice for gardening with kids to reward their interest in gardening with a fast payback.

Short-season vegetables:

arugula, lettuce (head), radishes, salad mix, spinach, turnips

What does this mean for garden planning?

These vegetables do best in cooler weather, so they should planted as early in the spring as possible. But if you plant only vegetables from this category, you'll have plenty of food to harvest in the beginning of the gardening season, but not much during the summer and early fall because they'll quit producing in the hot summer weather.

Many of the vegetables on this list can be replanted again in the late summer for fall and early winter harvest when the weather cools down again.

NOT SO QUICK TO HARVEST – Medium-Season Vegetables

These vegetables aren't as quick out of the starting gate as those above. You'll need to cultivate a little more patience while waiting for them to grow to harvest size. They're usually ready for the dinner table in 40-80 days. This is the largest category, and it features many of the late spring and mid-summer vegetables that we all know and love.

Medium-season vegetables:

beans (bush and pole), basil, beets, bok choy, broccoli, cabbage, carrots, cauliflower, cilantro, collards, corn, cucumber, dill, eggplant, fennel, kale, kohlrabi, okra, parsley, peas, peppers, potatoes, scallions, summer squash, swiss chard, tomatillos, tomatoes

What does this mean for garden planning?

This category makes up the bulk of what most of us grow in our gardens. If you grew only this category, you'd get the majority of your harvest during the summer. Try mixing in some short-season vegetables for food in the spring and long-season vegetables to extend the harvest into fall and early winter. This will give you a more well-rounded garden and a longer duration of harvests.

IT'S GOING TO TAKE A WHILE – Long-Season Vegetables

These vegetables are an investment in time, but often worth it.

They take their sweet time growing and developing, between 80–120 days until they're ready to harvest. These vegetables give us gardeners a new perspective on how long it actually takes to grow some of the food we see in the grocery store. Gardening requires a lot of patience!

Long-season vegetables:

asparagus, beans (dry), brussels sprouts, celery, dill (seed), edamame, garlic, leeks, melons, onions, parsnips, peppers (hot), potatoes, pumpkins, shallots, sweet potatoes, winter squash

What does this mean for garden planning?

If you grew only vegetables from this category, you'd have to wait until late summer and early fall before harvesting food from your garden. Mix in some short-and medium-season vegetables to ensure you have more months of harvests from your garden.

Dig In:

Take a look at the vegetables you selected on the **My Vegetable List** worksheet and see what harvest category they fall into. Make sure you're growing vegetables from all three categories.

You can now evaluate each vegetable according to all of the various characteristics we cover in this section. Use the **Veggie Essentials Cheat Sheet** at the back of the book to help you. Does the big picture effect which vegetables you'll choose to grow in your garden?

Once you start examining each vegetable more closely, you'll notice that different varieties of the same vegetable list varying days to harvest.

For example, Blue Wind broccoli is 49 days until harvest, while Belstar broccoli is 66 days until harvest.

If you want food sooner, pick a variety that matures more quickly. If you want to prolong your harvest, plant a few different varieties with a range of days to harvest.

Bringing It All Together

Now that we've looked at each vegetable from a variety of perspectives, what does it all mean?

First, in order to create a well-rounded garden with a longer harvest period, you'll want to choose vegetables from each of the various categories.

Secondly, since most of us don't have the room to grow everything we'd like in our gardens, it's important to strategically look at each vegetable and ask yourself, *"Do I think it's worth it to grow this in my garden?"* Considering all the facts about the vegetable, does it remain on your garden plan for the season?

To help you zoom out and take a critical look at each vegetable on your list, check out the **Veggie Essentials Cheat Sheet** at the end of the book. The categories we talked about in this section are organized into the first four columns of the chart. (We'll cover the rest of the columns in the next section of the book.) This is the time to start narrowing down what you want to grow this year.

Remember, this is a subjective exercise. Just because I think something's not worth it to grow in my garden (chard and cauliflower are top on my list!) doesn't mean you'll agree with me. It's the complete picture of each vegetable, along with your eating, cooking, and grocery shopping preferences that will help you choose whether you want to grow it or not.

And remember, you don't have to grow every vegetable each season.

I have a few vegetables on my list (okra, cabbage, edamame) that I don't plant every year because they're not my priority vegetables. But, I do think they're fun to grow periodically, so they're on a two- to three-year rotation instead.

There's a certain amount of trial and error in this process (and all of gardening!). The experimentation is one of the things that makes gardening so much fun. And because it's cyclical, we get to try completely new and different experiments every single season.

As you go forward in your garden planning, I encourage you to approach it with a strategic eye mixed with a sense of curiosity and adventure. This ensures you'll always be having fun and learning!

BONUS VIDEO: Watch a quick video where I share more about how I make decisions about what to grow in my garden each year. creativevegetablegardener.com/smart-planning-book

When we hold a seed or plant in our hands, it can feel like anything is a possibility in our gardens at that point in time.

It's amazing that a tiny seed will swell and sprout and eventually grow into an earthy orange carrot, a towering tomato plant, or a sprawling cucumber vine. We can't have a garden without seeds and plants; they're what make our gardens literally spring to life.

Now that you're honing in on exactly what you want to grow in your garden this year, the next step is to make sure you have the seeds and plants you need when the garden season arrives. It can be confusing to know when to order seeds or plants, which varieties to grow, and how much to order. You'll be sorting through these questions and more in this section. At the end, you'll have a completed shopping list and be ready to order your seeds for the season.

You're going to be such an organized gardener this year!

Know When to Plant a Seed or a Plant

Imagine yourself out in your garden ready to plant. Some days this will mean opening a sparkling new seed packet and gently placing the seeds into their new home in the soil. At other times, you'll coax a plant out of its pot and dig it a nice roomy hole where it can set down roots.

These are two very different ways of planting vegetables: with a **seed** or with a **plant**.

Some vegetables do best when they're planted in the garden as seeds, and some fare better as plants. When you have a plan for how you're going to plant each vegetable, you'll be able to set yourself up for success by making sure you have the supplies you need on hand when the garden season rolls around.

VEGETABLES PLANTED BY SEED

Taking a seed directly out of the packet and planting it right into your garden bed is called direct seeding. If you've ever grown green beans, carrots, or spinach, you've likely planted them in your garden this way.

There are various reasons why vegetables are direct seeded. Some vegetable seed is very inexpensive and reliable, so you know it has a good chance of germinating in many different conditions—radishes and green beans are a good example. Some vegetables don't like it when their roots are disturbed, so planting a seedling isn't a good idea. It makes sense that root crops fall into this category, such as carrots, beets, and turnips.

Direct seeding allows you to plant a large space of the garden very quickly and easily. And not having to start and care for the plants in your house cuts down on the work involved in growing these vegetables.

But newly seeded vegetables need a lot of initial attention. You'll need to make sure the garden bed stays consistently moist until the seeds germinate. That means you'll need to keep the garden bed watered if you're not getting rain.

Newly germinated seeds have very tiny leaves, so they're often more vulnerable to insects and pests. They also don't compete with weeds well. You'll often notice that the weeds are growing at the same rate as the vegetables.

So, if you're someone who is unable to pay close attention to your garden, you may want to consider growing more transplanted vegetables instead of direct-seeded ones.

Direct-seeded vegetables:

arugula, all beans, beets, carrots, cilantro, corn, dill, garlic, edamame, parsnip, peas, potatoes, radishes, salad mix, spinach, turnips

VEGETABLES PLANTED BY PLANT

When you take a vegetable plant, dig a hole in the soil, and plant it into your garden, it's called transplanting. The vegetable plant is usually called a seedling. It's a baby plant grown from seed by you in your home or by a nursery or farmer in a greenhouse.

Why do we transplant some vegetables instead of direct seeding them? Gardeners who live in colder climates with shorter seasons often start their plants inside to give them a head start. This ensures they'll have enough time to grow to full size once they're outside in the garden. Peppers, eggplant, and tomatoes fall into this category.

Some vegetable seeds, like peppers, herbs, and many flowers, take extra care to germinate. It would be difficult to give them the attention they need in the changing conditions of the garden, so it's easier to either start the seeds inside or buy plants. I often struggle with getting pepper seeds to germinate in my house even with a heating mat, so I can't imagine how difficult it would be if I direct seeded them!

Seedlings make it easy to measure out the spacing between plants in your garden. This is especially important if you're trying to grow as much food in your garden as possible. You also won't need to go back and thin out dense plantings like you sometimes do with direct-seeded vegetables.

Transplanted vegetables:

asparagus, basil, broccoli, brussels sprouts, cabbage, cauliflower, celery, collards, eggplant, garlic chives, kale, leeks, marjoram, mint, onion, onion chives, oregano, parsley, peppers, raspberries, rhubarb, rosemary, sage, shallots, strawberries, sweet potatoes, tarragon, thyme, tomatillos, tomatoes

What does this mean for garden planning?

If you're growing any of the transplanted vegetables in your garden this season, you'll need to make sure you have the seedlings ready to go when it's time to plant. If you start your own seeds at home, you'll grow the plants yourself. If not, then you'll need to buy them from a local farmers' market or nursery. We talk more about growing your own plants at home on pg. 82.

PLANT OR SEED . . . IT'S YOUR CHOICE!

There are a few vegetables that will do just fine whether they're direct seeded or transplanted, so it's ultimately your choice.

Keep in mind that planting seedlings can give you a jump start on the season. Instead of waiting for seeds to germinate in the garden, you can skip over that waiting period and plant a seedling instead.

For example, I like to grow a few kohlrabi in my garden in spring. I want them to grow to harvest size as quickly as possible, because I'm starved for fresh vegetables at that time of year. So, I start them by seed in my house in late winter and transplant the seedlings into the garden in spring even though they grow just fine when direct seeded.

Since I'm giving them a head start of at least a month in the house, because it's still too cold to plant them directly into the garden, I'm able to harvest my first kohlrabi a week (or several weeks) earlier than I would if I'd planted them directly into the garden in spring.

Vegetables grown by plant or seed:

bok choy, cucumber, fennel, kohlrabi, lettuce (head), melons, okra, pumpkins, scallions, summer squash, swiss chard, winter squash

What does this mean for garden planning?

Take the list of vegetables you're planning to grow this year and figure out how each one is planted. Use the "Direct Seed or Transplant" column on the **Veggie Essentials Cheat Sheet** as a reference. Then, use the **Seed & Plant Shopping List** to keep track of which seeds you to need to order, which plants you need to start at home, and which plants you're going to buy. Don't worry about variety or amount just yet, we'll talk about that later.

Something to consider: Direct-seeded vegetables call for more attention right after planting. Seeds waiting to germinate need to remain consistently moist. They must be watered every one to two days until germination, which can be anywhere from a few days to several weeks.

If you're just starting out as a new gardener, it may be easier to plant seedlings instead of seeds. If you don't think you'll have time to give direct-seeded vegetables the attention they need to germinate, consider just growing things you can plant as seedlings for the first year.

You can print out a copy of this worksheet at creativevegetablegardener.com/smart-planning-book.

SEED & PLANT SHOPPING LIST

SEEDS TO ORDER			
Vegetable	Variety	Amount	Notes

PLANTS TO START AT HOME

Vegetable	Variety	Amount	Notes

PLANTS TO BUY

Vegetable	Variety	Amount	Notes

Break Open Those Seed Catalogs

Hopefully you've been eagerly checking your mailbox the last few weeks and have been delighted by the arrival of your new, shiny, and colorful seed catalogs. Now it's time to really dig into the possibilities they offer!

This is a great activity for a dreary and cold winter day. Make another cup of your favorite tea or coffee, cozy up in a comfy chair (or spread out on your dining room table), and spend some time dreaming about the colorful and beautiful food you'll grow in your garden this season.

But first, a word of caution! It can be very overwhelming to start flipping through a pile of seed catalogs. There's a good chance you might go from excited to stressed out in a very short amount of time.

To keep yourself focused, revisit your answers on the **What Do I Want to Grow?** worksheet to remind you of your priorities for shopping, cooking, and eating. Use your **Seed & Plant Shopping List** to help you compile your seed order.

In the following pages, we'll break down the seed-ordering process into more manageable steps. I'll make sure you understand what you should be looking at and thinking about when you're gathering your seed order together.

And remember, this is the fun part, so relax and enjoy it!

Understanding Different Types of Seeds

A lot of different terms and phrases get thrown around when people start talking about seeds. To help you make your own educated decisions, here are a few definitions you'll want to be familiar with as you dig through your catalogs.

Organic seeds (in the US) have been grown in a field according to USDA-certified organic standards. The certification process includes inspection of farm fields, processes, and records to ensure the farm is following the standards set forth by the USDA, such as no synthetic fertilizers, pesticides, or fungicides. Many seed catalogs offer organic and non-organic seeds for the same variety.

If you have an organic garden, buying organic seeds makes sense because the seeds are grown under similar conditions as your garden. Organic seed is sometimes more expensive than conventional seed. If there's more demand from consumers, the price will drop over time.

Hybrid seeds are the result of crossing two different parent plants by hand in a controlled environment. They are bred to select for certain characteristics like color, sweetness, disease resistance, and uniformity.

These seeds are often referred to as F1 hybrids. Some seed catalogs, like Johnny's, put F1 in the vegetable listing to let you know that it's a hybrid. People who save their own garden seeds dislike hybrids because saving the seed results in an unpredictable mix of the ancestral plants.

But some of the most popular garden vegetables are hybrids like Sungold Tomato, Burpee Big Boy Tomato, and two of my favorites: Carmen Pepper and Dancer Eggplant. Hybrids are a part of most farms and gardens because some sometimes they're the best-performing varieties out there.

Heirloom seeds have been handed down from one generation to another over time. There's no exact definition of how old a seed needs to be to be considered an heirloom, although some sources state 40-50 years. All heirloom plants are open-pollinated, but not all open-pollinated plants are heirlooms. (See below.)

Heirloom varieties are not often found in the larger commercial market because of various characteristics that sometimes make the vegetables unsuitable for large-scale production—lack of uniformity, short shelf life, or difficulty in transporting them long distances.   The seed company Seed Savers Exchange sells only heirloom varieties.

Heirloom varieties are often unique and come with interesting histories about the people and families that grew them. The number of vegetable varieties available in the global market has shrunk over time as the biggest seed companies have consolidated. Growing heirlooms is a way to help preserve the genetic diversity of our food supply.

Open-pollinated seeds are a result of pollination occurring by insect, bird, wind, humans, or other natural mechanisms. Because pollen flows freely between individual plants, open-pollinated plants are more genetically diverse. This can cause a greater amount of variation within plant populations, which allows plants to slowly adapt to local growing conditions and climate year-to-year.

All open-pollinated varieties are not heirlooms, since there are new open-pollinated varieties being introduced to the market.

Gardeners who save their own seeds use open-pollinated varieties because the seeds (with some special monitoring to prevent cross-pollination) will produce the same variety year after year. Hybrids, which are a cross between two parents, will likely revert back to one of those parents if you save the seed, so they won't be consistent year to year.

Even if you're not a seed saver, you may already be growing popular open-pollinated varieties like Kentucky Wonder pole bean, Scarlet Nantes carrot, California Wonder pepper, and Brandywine tomato.

Genetically Modified Organisms, or GMO seeds, have been altered using genetic engineering. Genetic engineering involves the deletion or insertion of genes, usually from a different species, to engineer specific traits such as resistance to pest and herbicides, improved shelf life, or increased nutritional value.

They are subject to intellectual property law, so it's illegal to save seed. Most common garden vegetables are not GMOs, mostly because the focus has been on the larger global agricultural market.

As a gardener, you may be aware of the many different viewpoints in this larger conversation about seeds and our global and national seed supply. These are complicated issues, and I encourage you to do some more reading and form your own educated opinion.

If you feel strongly about buying seeds from sources that do not carry GMO seed of any kind, you can find a list of companies that have signed the Safe Seed Pledge at councilforresponsiblegenetics.org.

In my own garden, I grow a mix of heirloom, open-pollinated, and hybrid seed, and I try to buy organic whenever it's available because it aligns with my values. I've tested a lot of varieties in my garden over the years and the number one thing I look at is performance. Does it produce a lot of food, stand up to common diseases, and taste good? I don't really care if a variety is an heirloom, a hybrid, or open-pollinated as long as it produces food for me and my family.

I also like to grow beautiful vegetables, so I evaluate each variety from that point of view as well. But, it needs to perform well and taste delicious first, and be attractive as a bonus.

I love growing sweet peppers, so I've experimented with many different varieties over the years. Many of them haven't passed my performance test, so I don't grow them again. But the varieties that are on my favorites list are a mix of the above categories: Carmen pepper, a hybrid, Jimmy Nardello, an heirloom, and Lively Yellow, an open-pollinated variety.

The most important thing to remember is to keep track of the varieties you plant in your garden each year so that you can repeat your successes and ditch the failures. Over time you'll compile your own personal list of favorite varieties that perform well in your garden year after year.

HIGH MOWING
Organic Seeds

Corno di Toro
Sweet Pepper

Heirloom | 70 days green, 78 red
1/64 ounce | item: 2778-A

USDA ORGANIC

PEPPER

SANTA FE GRANDE

Satisfaction Guaranteed

EggPlant Turkish Orange

VERY SWEET AND FLAVORFUL

BAKER CREEK HEIRLOOM SEEDS
MANSFIELD ✷ MISSOURI 65704

Pepper Yellow Monster

VERY IMPRESSIVE FRUIT

BAKER CREEK HEIRLOOM SEEDS
MANSFIELD ✷ MISSOURI 65704

BROCCOLI

DE CICCO

Satisfaction Guaranteed

HIGH MOWING
Organic Seeds

White Russian
Kale

Open Pollinated | 30 days baby, 65 full size
1/32 ounce | sows ~ 23 ft | item: 2528-A

USDA ORGANIC

How to Read a Seed Catalog

Flipping through a seed catalog can be confusing because there's so much information listed in there! Who knew there was so much to say about vegetable seeds?

The good news is this: although the layouts of the various seed company catalogs are different, they basically list the same kinds of information. Let's take a quick look at an example listing for the best cherry tomato out there, Sun Gold.

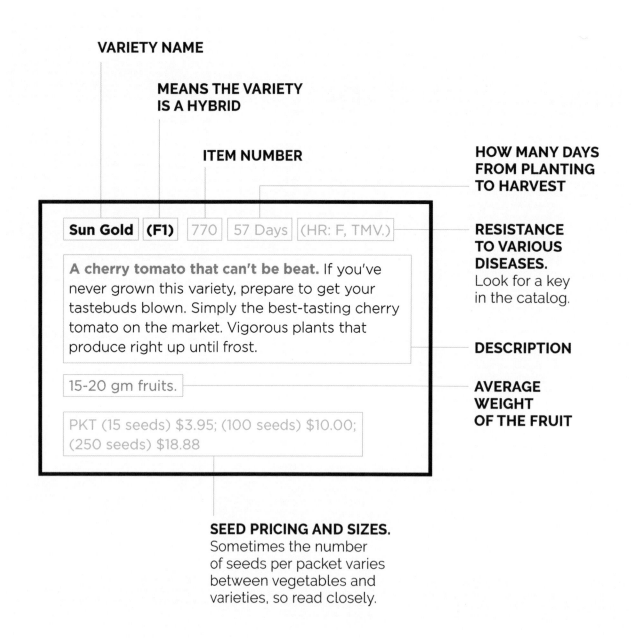

VARIETY NAME

MEANS THE VARIETY IS A HYBRID

ITEM NUMBER

HOW MANY DAYS FROM PLANTING TO HARVEST

| Sun Gold | (F1) | 770 | 57 Days | (HR: F, TMV.) |

RESISTANCE TO VARIOUS DISEASES. Look for a key in the catalog.

A cherry tomato that can't be beat. If you've never grown this variety, prepare to get your tastebuds blown. Simply the best-tasting cherry tomato on the market. Vigorous plants that produce right up until frost.

DESCRIPTION

15-20 gm fruits.

AVERAGE WEIGHT OF THE FRUIT

PKT (15 seeds) $3.95; (100 seeds) $10.00; (250 seeds) $18.88

SEED PRICING AND SIZES. Sometimes the number of seeds per packet varies between vegetables and varieties, so read closely.

Choose the Best Varieties for Your Garden

Once you start looking through your seed catalogs you might start to get overwhelmed with all the varieties out there. There are thousands of varieties of tomatoes out in the world. How do you choose?

Throughout my years of gardening I've learned that not all varieties are created equal. What variety you plant can be the difference between success and failure. And just because a variety performs well in my home garden in Wisconsin doesn't mean it will be as productive in a garden in Washington or Georgia.

There's going to be some trial and error to find what you like and what performs well in your garden. That's why it's important to keep records of what you plant each year so you can repeat the successes and ditch the failures. If you haven't been having success with a certain vegetable in your garden, try a different variety this season.

The farmers in your local area can be a great source of information and advice. They do a lot of trialing of different varieties from year to year, and CSA farmers in particular are focused on finding great-performing vegetable varieties since they grow them for a living. If you have a farmer you patronize at your local market each week, consider asking her for variety recommendations.

For several years, I was having a terrible time growing Brussels sprouts. One of the local CSA farmers kept bringing beautiful Brussels sprouts to his stand each week. One day I stopped by and asked him which variety he grew. We chatted a bit about the challenges of growing Brussels sprouts and he was happy to share his wisdom with me. Now I grow the same variety he does and have had much better success!

I've trialed a lot of varieties in my garden over the years and love to share my recommendations. You can find them in the **Veggie Essentials Cheat Sheet** next to each individual vegetable. I also share ten of my favorite unique and colorful varieties in the following pages.

What does this mean for garden planning?

If you've been having mixed success with a certain vegetable, ask around in your local community to find out what varieties other gardeners and farmers are having success with. It's imperative that you keep records each season so that you can repeat your successes and stay away from the varieties that have failed.

It takes a while to learn when failure is due to the variety or to user error! That's why I recommend growing several different varieties of each vegetable in your garden. If you plant five tomatoes, don't plant five of the same variety. It's better to plant two to three different varieties. If they all fail, it might be something you're doing wrong. If one doesn't grow well, but the other two go gangbusters, then it's likely the variety and not you.

BONUS VIDEO: Watch a video where I share more tips on ordering your seeds at creativevegetablegardener.com/ smart-planning-book

Tips for Ordering Seeds

The longer you wait to place your seed order, the bigger the chance you'll miss out on some of the best varieties out there. Seeds do sell out, so order yours early. I usually place my seed order in early to mid-February.

Again, try growing more than one variety for each vegetable. This allows you to compare the growth and performance of the varieties, and to find your new favorites more quickly. Don't put all your eggs in one basket!

Unless you have a very big garden, the smallest-sized seed packet for each vegetable is likely an adequate amount. There are a few things that I plant a lot of in my garden, like carrots and spinach, so I often purchase the next size up for these vegetables. Quantities vary among the various seed companies, so check to make sure you know how many are in the packet before you order it.

Clean out your current seed stash before ordering seeds for the upcoming season. Throw out anything that's over two or three years old. Don't waste time with seeds that might not germinate. It's better to buy new seeds than to try to get by with old ones.

If one of your goals is to store and preserve more food for off season use, look for phrases like "storage variety" or "good for preserving" in the seed catalog descriptions. For example, if you want to make a lot of tomato sauce for winter, you might choose to grow Amish Paste. In the Seed Savers Exchange catalog description it says this variety is "excellent for sauce."

Pay attention to the descriptions in the catalog. If you live in a cold climate choose varieties that are listed as growing well in short-season areas. If you live in a warm climate, buy seeds that perform well in hot weather or long seasons.

Ten Unique and Colorful Varieties to Grow

Red tomatoes, green beans, and orange carrots are great, but there's so much more out there! This season, take a chance and grow some unique and interesting varieties in your garden. Growing beautiful and colorful food dramatically increases the fun you'll have in your garden.

Pulling an amazing rainbow of carrots out of the ground in summer, looking out your window and seeing jewel-toned flowers bopping their heads in the wind, and adding vegetables that aren't only tasty, but also gorgeous, to your evening meals are all joys that should be a part of every gardener's lifestyle.

If you're ready to create a garden that feeds your body and your soul, add some of these favorites to your seed order this year.

Jimmy Nardello's Pepper

Lively Yellow Pepper

Scarlet Kale

Golden Sweet Peas

Yellow & Chioggia Beets

Purple Ruffles Basil

Purple Viking Potato

Deep Purple Carrot

Dragon Tongue Bean

Dancer Eggplant

Want to see more recommended varieties? Check out the **Veggie Essentials Cheat Sheet** at the end of the book.

Dig In:

Your next step is to get your seed order together. Use the tips on the previous pages, the recommended varieties on the **Veggie Essentials Cheat Sheet**, and my **Ten Unique and Colorful Varieties** to get you started. As you make decisions about which varieties you're going to order, fill them in on your **Seed & Plant Shopping List** .

Planting for Beauty with Flowers

A common complaint about vegetables gardens is that they're not very attractive. I couldn't disagree more! At my house my vegetable gardens are front and center—an integral part of my home landscape.

Over the years I've learned I can have a garden that produces a lot of food and is also beautiful to look at. And you can, too!

The simplest thing you can do to elevate your garden from a place where you grow food to an attractive part of your overall home landscape is to add flowers. If you start your own vegetable seedlings at home, think about ordering some flower seed this year and starting them alongside the vegetables.

Or, make a visit to a local nursery in spring and buy a flat of colorful annual flowers. Annual flowers are the perfect companion to vegetables since they have a very similar lifespan. You can plant perennials in your vegetable garden, but keep in mind they will stay in place year after year and may be difficult to work around.

I like annuals because once they get going, they tend to bloom for most of the season, and then they die back with the first frosts. This allows me to clear them out of my garden at the same time I'm cleaning out my vegetable plants. An added benefit of planting flowers among your vegetables is their blooms will attract beneficial insects and pollinators, which are an important part of a balanced organic garden.

This season, reserve some space at the end of some of your garden beds and tuck some flowers in amongst the vegetables. And don't be afraid to mix and match flowers; the color combinations add an extra layer of beauty and interest to your vegetable garden.

Six Favorite Flowers for the Vegetable Garden

Shopping for flowers for your vegetable garden can be as simple as taking a trip to your local nursery and seeing what catches your eye. I usually buy a flat of mixed annuals each spring and spread them throughout my garden. I have a list of favorite annuals I always grow, and then I experiment with new varieties I pick up from the nursery each season in the hopes of finding my new favorite flower!

State Fair Zinnia

Lady in Red Salvia

Blue Victoria Salvia

Prairie Sun Rudbeckia

Verbena Bonariensis

Strawberry Fields Globe Amaranth

Eight Steps for Ordering Seeds

This is the part you've been waiting for! It's time to order your seeds. Let's get you back into your favorite comfy chair with that cup of tea on a cold winter day. There's no better way to spend a cloudy weekend afternoon than perusing seed catalogs and dreaming about your garden.

Not sure where to start? It can be overwhelming, so I thought I'd share with you how I go about ordering seeds for my own garden.

STEP 1: I use the **Plant & Seed Shopping List** to write down all of the vegetables I want to grow. I don't worry about variety just yet, unless I know there's something I'll definitely grow this season.

STEP 2: I sit down with the seed catalogs and a pen and circle everything that catches my eye. This is my dreaming, fun phase so anything is a possibility at this point. I know I'll drastically whittle it down from here later.

STEP 3: Throughout the year when I see or read about a variety I might want to try out in my garden, I save it to a special Pinterest board. After I look through my seed catalogs I'll revisit that list to remind myself what has caught my eye over the last year. You can check out my collection here. https://www.pinterest.com/createveggies/ garden-plants-i-want-to-try/

STEP 4: I take out the small plastic tub where I store my seeds and sort through them. Most seeds remain viable for 2-3 years, depending on how they're stored. I discard any seed packets that are older than that because I don't want to take the chance they won't germinate or produce well.

STEP 5: I break out my garden binder and consult my planting map from last year to refresh my memory of what I planted and how many of each vegetable I grew. I often take notes on the map of things I don't want to forget as I'm planning my garden next year.

STEP 6: Finally, I'll go back to the seed catalogs and start to make my final selections. I'll consult my garden map from last year and my piles of leftover seed packets to help me decide what seeds and how many of each I need for this season. I usually work through each vegetable one at a time so I don't get overwhelmed.

STEP 7: I place my orders on the various companies' websites. I don't wait too long to submit my order because some popular varieties get sold out each year. I usually order from two to three seed companies since no one company has all of the varieties I like.

STEP 8: I sit back and wait for the seeds to arrive in my mailbox. Or, if it's close to seed starting season, I start to dig out my supplies and get them organized.

Starting Vegetable Plants at Home

There are many reasons to start growing your own vegetable plants at home. The #1 reason? It's so much fun! In late winter, when many of us are wishing we could get back out into our gardens, we can get busy digging our hands into the soil and playing with seeds in our own home. There's nothing quite like watching your vegetable plants grow to start getting you excited for the upcoming season.

Growing your own plants can also save you money in your garden budget, especially if you have a big garden. Each year I plant 30-40 sweet pepper plants. If I went to the farmers' market to buy them at $2 a pop, that would be $60-80 just for pepper seedlings! I also grow hundreds of other vegetables in my garden each season.

When you shop at the nursery and farmers' market for plants, you might notice that everyone is selling the same familiar varieties. And sometimes they're not very exciting. When you grow your own plants from seed, you can order unusual and colorful varieties and try new things every year.

One of the most enjoyable aspects of the gardening process is the constant learning and building of your skills.

Learning to start your own plants adds another tool to your gardening toolkit. It takes a little bit of time and money to get your system set up, but once you master the basics, it's an easily repeatable process each year.

Depending on where you live and what you're growing in your garden, you'll likely be starting your seeds anywhere from January through April. My eBook, *Super Easy Seed Starting*, breaks down the entire process step by step to help save you time and money, gives you the confidence you need to get started growing your vegetable plants, and helps you skip over the most common mistakes made by seed starters. You can find out more at creativevegetablegardener.com/seed-starting

Where to Buy Plants

If you've decided you're not going to start seeds this season, or even if you plan to start some plants and buy some plants, then you'll have some plant shopping to do come spring. There are a few things to consider before you rush out with your wallet to your local nursery or farmers' market.

At the local Garden Expo one winter, while chatting with some fellow gardeners, they mentioned their terrible luck with peppers during the last season—their fruit didn't ripen to red. I asked what variety they grew. They looked at each other and shrugged, replying, *"We don't know. We just bought plants from the local big box store."*

We all have times when we cut corners in the garden. But buying vegetable starts is not the place to do so. When I was a beginning gardener, I thought all varieties of one vegetable were pretty much the same. Especially with things like broccoli, cabbage, and orange carrots, since there's not much observable difference between the varieties. I would just go to the local store selling seeds and seedlings and buy a handful of what looked good. I often had mixed results and wasn't sure why.

It wasn't until I started working on vegetable farms that I realized how much time and effort farmers put into selecting varieties that perform well in their fields. A pepper is not a pepper is not a pepper.

Variety does matter.

And because variety can mean the difference between success and failure, where you buy your plants really does matter.

So, where should you buy your seedlings this year? From a local vegetable farmer.

Buying from someone who is growing those same varieties with success in your area means the plants are more likely to produce a bumper crop for you, too. You can also ask the farmer questions, get growing tips, and even ask for suggestions for her own personal favorites.

Stay away from the big box store when it comes to buying vegetable plants! The seedlings sold there are not necessarily selected to do well in your local climate. The variety might be more acclimated to a garden in Texas than one in Wisconsin. Those are two very different worlds!

Many days pass between the moment we tuck a seedling into the ground and harvest time. Gardening is quite an investment in time, so it's worth the effort to seek out varieties that are more likely to succeed in your local conditions. This year, go to your local farmers' market, find a vegetable farmer, and ask questions about the plants before you buy them. I bet you'll experience a higher level of success in your garden as a result.

When to Buy Plants

The downtown farmers' market in Madison, where I live, starts in mid-April each year. After a long, dark, and cold winter, we Madisonians burst out of our houses and rush to the market to soak in the sights, sounds, and colors of the early spring. It's a wonderful yearly tradition, this first market of the year, but more often than not the weather is still pretty cold at this time of year.

Regardless of the weather, the farmers at the market are starting to sell some vegetable plants for home gardeners. While making the rounds I often spy things like tomato, pepper, and eggplant seedlings for sale, and shoppers carrying around these plants.

The problem is that in Madison, you can't plant those warm weather vegetables for at least another month. We often have frosts through mid-May, and these plants are not frost hardy. There's no sense in buying a plant a full month before you can plant it because you're going to have to take care of it that whole time.

The best time to buy a seedling is right before you're going to plant it. Let the farmer who grew it and knows how to take care of it keep it in her possession for as long as possible. Young seedlings have special light and heat needs that are difficult to replicate at home unless you have your own seed starting set-up.

This means that you may have to make a few shopping trips for plants. You'll need to buy your cool weather vegetable plants (lettuce, broccoli, kale) weeks earlier than you buy your warm weather vegetables (basil, tomatoes, egpplant), since they go into the garden weeks apart.

The best way to figure out when to buy your plants is to figure out when you're going to plant them in your garden. I'll help you create your own spring planting calendar in the next section.

WHEN & HOW TO PLANT YOUR GARDEN

In the previous sections of this book, you've taken a look at your cooking and eating habits, thought about the role you want your garden to play in your life, learned more about the different characteristics of each vegetable, decided what you want to grow this season, and placed your seed order. You've made a ton of progress!

Now that you're ready for the gardening season to begin, you might be asking yourself, "How do I know when to start planting?"

When you start planting seeds and plants depends upon where you live and what the spring weather is like in your local region. A gardener in Georgia will have a very different timeline than a gardener in Michigan. Your next step in the garden-planning process is to figure out when you'll plant each vegetable in your garden this spring.

Create Your Spring Planting Schedule

When I first started gardening over fifteen years ago I was put in charge of a community herb garden with a friend of mine. We were both relatively new to gardening and decided to meet for a planning session to figure out how we would approach that first season.

After deciding what we wanted to grow, the next thing we did was map out a planting schedule to guide us through what to do each week of the gardening season. Little did I know that this would be my first of many planting schedules. I still have the old homemade notebook with my neatly written out schedule for that season!

Having a planting schedule for your garden is one of the best ways to get the most food possible because it keeps you on track. It's like a little nudge each week to get out there and get planting!

If you live in a short season area like I do in Wisconsin, it's important to plant early and often so that you maximize the gardening season with frequent and abundant harvests. The delicious food we harvest from our gardens for dinner is what makes gardening so worth it, right?

To create your own planting calendar, your first step is to figure out your **average last frost date**. The best way to do this is to go to the website plantmaps.com and enter in your zip code. It will pull up information for your area including your average last frost. It lists a date range, so if you want to be on the safe side you can pick a date at the end of the range for your last frost.

If you're my neighbor in Wisconsin, you can go to wisconline.com/counties and select your county to display your median last frost date.

I've found that the last frost dates you find online can sometimes differ a bit from one another, so consider consulting several different sources and then deciding what date to pick for your last frost. One of the best sources of this information is your local county extension office. Keep in mind that the actual day of the last frost can vary widely from year to year, especially with changing climate conditions.

My average last frost date: _____

Now that you've figured out your average last frost, it's time to create your personal planting schedule. Grab a calendar and the **Spring Planting Schedule** worksheet. Fill in your average last frost date at the top of the worksheet.

Then, use your calendar to count backwards from your last frost date to fill in the rest of the dates on the Planting Schedule. This will help you calculate when you should be planting each vegetable in your garden.

You can find an example of one I filled out for my garden at creativevegetablegardener.com/smart-planning-book

You may notice that some vegetables are listed more than once on the calendar. These are great for succession planting! Succession planting means planting a vegetable several times throughout the season for a more continual supply.

For example, instead of planting an entire bed full of beets, which will all be ready for harvest at about the same time, you can plant a small row of beets every two to three weeks in spring so you have a more gradual harvest, not a huge deluge at one time.

If you have a small garden or don't want to use succession planting, you can plant the vegetables that are listed multiple times on any of the weeks they're listed.

The vegetables are also divided between direct seed and transplant to help you figure out whether you'll be planting each one by seed or by plant. If you're not sure what that means, refer to **Know When to Plant a Seed or a Plant** on page 54.

What does this mean for garden planning?

Having a planting schedule helps you figure out what you should be doing in the garden each week in spring. But, remember, it's important to keep notes on when you plant each vegetable so you can tweak your planting schedule over time to fit your individual situation.

Some of the cold weather vegetables like spinach and lettuce benefit from being planted as early as possible because they don't do well in the hotter weather of late spring and summer.

Planting doesn't stop six weeks after your last frost. I continue to plant in my garden up until 4-6 weeks before my first frost in fall. But that's a topic for another book!

 SMART TIP
The suggested dates for planting are a guideline.

You may need to tweak them to fit the climate of your garden. Remember, any vegetables you're planting after your average last frost are not very cold tolerant. Make sure you always check the weather before planting anything in your garden, and pay special attention to the extended forecast. If there is any chance of temperatures in the mid- to low-thirties F, hold off on planting vegetables that can't survive a frost.

It's better to plant a little later in the month than lose an entire vegetable bed to a late frost. (Been there, done that. It's terrible.)

You can print out a copy of this worksheet at creativevegetablegardener.com/smart-planning-book.

SPRING PLANTING SCHEDULE

My average last frost date: _____

4 WEEKS BEFORE LAST FROST		DATE:	
DIRECT SEED	Arugula	Radish	
	Beets	Potatoes	
	Carrots	Salad Mix	
	Cilantro	Spinach	
	Dill	Swiss Chard (or transplant)	
	Kohlrabi (or transplant)	Turnips	
	Peas	Other Greens, i.g. Asian greens	
TRANSPLANT	Asparagus	Raspberries	
	Bok Choy (or direct seed)	Rhubarb	
	Broccoli	Scallions (or direct seed)	
	Collards	Shallots	
	Kale	Strawberries	
	Leeks	Perennial Herbs: Garlic Chives, Marjoram, Onion Chives, Oregano, Parsley, Sage, Tarragon, Thyme	
	Lettuce Heads (or direct seed)		
	Onions		

2 WEEKS BEFORE LAST FROST		DATE:	
DIRECT SEED	Arugula	Potatoes	
	Beets	Radish	
	Carrots	Salad Mix	
	Cilantro	Spinach	
	Dill	Turnips	
	Parsnip	Other greens	
TRANSPLANT	Bok Choy (or direct seed)	Fennel	
	Broccoli	Kohlrabi (or direct seed)	
	Brussels Sprouts	Lettuce Heads (or direct seed)	
	Cabbage	Salad Mix	
	Cauliflower	Scallions (or direct seed)	

LAST FROST WEEK: Check the 10-day forecast and don't plant summer vegetables if there's a chance of frost.		**Date:**	
DIRECT SEED	Beans	Potatoes	
	Beets	Radish	
	Carrots	Salad Mix	
	Cilantro	Spinach	
	Dill	Turnips	
	Parsnip		
TRANSPLANT	Basil	Peppers	
	Bok Choy	Rosemary	
	Broccoli	Summer Squash (or direct seed)	
	Cauliflower	Tomatoes	
	Cucumber (or direct seed)	Tomatillos	
	Eggplant		

2 WEEKS AFTER LAST FROST		**Date:**	
DIRECT SEED	Beans	Parsnip	
	Beets	Potatoes	
	Carrots	Pumpkins (or transplant)	
	Celery	Radish	
	Corn	Salad Mix	
	Cucumber	Summer Squash	
	Edamame	Winter Squash (or transplant)	
TRANSPLANT	Basil	Melons (or direct seed)	
	Broccoli	Okra	
	Lettuce Heads	Sweet Potatoes	

4 WEEKS AFTER LAST FROST		**Date:**	
DIRECT SEED	Beans	Cucumber	
	Beets	Corn	
	Carrots	Potatoes	
	Cilantro	Summer Squash	
TRANSPLANT	Basil	Scallions	
	Lettuce Heads		

6 WEEKS AFTER LAST FROST		Date:	
DIRECT SEED	Beans	Cucumber	
	Beets	Summer Squash	
	Carrots		
TRANSPLANT	Basil	Scallions	
	Lettuce Heads		

How to Space Your Plants

Exactly how to space your plants in the garden can be confusing. Information on the internet, on seed packets, and in books is often conflicting. If you plant things too close together, they won't have room to grow to full size, but when you plant them too far apart, you end up with a lot of wasted space in your garden that could otherwise be producing food.

If you've ever visited a vegetable farm, you know that most farmers plant their vegetables in rows down the length of the farm beds. This is because it's the most efficient way to grow vegetables in large amounts when you're using machinery.

Your garden is likely not the size of your local vegetable farm, so you have some leeway in how you plant your vegetables. Planting in rows is probably the easiest way to grow vegetables in your own garden, but it's not necessarily the most attractive way. And by now you know that in addition to creating a garden that produces a lot of food, I also like to teach gardeners how to have a beautiful garden.

So, first we'll talk about how to plant in rows, and then I'll give you some other options in case you want to mix it up a bit!

The following **Vegetable Spacing Guide** is meant to be just what it sounds like—a guide. There's no replacement for your own observation, so make sure you're keeping notes on the spacing in your garden so you can make changes when necessary.

The guide breaks down the vegetables into the direct seeded and transplanted categories we talked about on pg. 54.

TRANSPLANTED VEGETABLE SPACING

For transplanted vegetables, you'll be planting a seedling into your garden. This is a convenient way to get the exact spacing you want between your plants because you can measure it out.

Let's take broccoli as an example. On the spacing guide it says to plant broccoli plants in two rows with 12" between each plant. If you have a rectangular garden bed, you'll plant the broccoli in two rows down the length of the bed and make sure there is 12" between each seedling.

4' x 8' RAISED BED

BROCCOLI

I use an old measuring tape to help me space my seedlings. I've realized over time that I'm not so accurate with estimating the spacing in my garden. A measuring tape allows me to make sure I'm squeezing the most plants possible into a bed, while also allowing them the space they need to grow to full size.

When you're planting your seedlings, make sure you're staggering the plants in the rows to give them the most space possible. In the drawing on the previous page you can see how the broccoli plants are spaced in a triangular pattern, so that each plant can stretch out and not interfere with the plant next to it.

If you're only planting six broccoli plants and they don't take up your whole garden bed, you can fill in the rest of the bed with another vegetable. You can continue with two rows of kale, or three rows of seeded carrots, or four rows of spinach. You can feel free to mix vegetables together in the same bed. Just keep records so you can make sure to rotate what's planted in each garden bed every season.

4 ROWS CARROTS

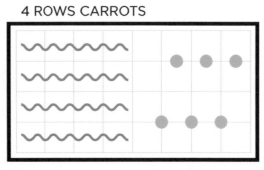

6 BROCCOLI

If your garden doesn't have defined beds and paths, then it's time to create a more permanent garden design.

Having established beds and paths in your garden creates a more structured garden, makes maintenance much easier over the long term, and allows you to focus your energy in the garden beds themselves and not on areas that are paths.

To learn more about how and why to make a permanent design, check out the bonus at creativevegetablegardener.com/smart-planning-book.

DIRECT SEEDED VEGETABLE SPACING

Direct seeding vegetables is very straightforward. There are two spacing guidelines you'll want to keep in mind—the distance between each seed as you put it into the soil, and the space between the rows of vegetables. For the space between each seed, I simply follow the recommendations on the seed packet. But, for the space between the rows, I've found that the various seed packets suggest different spacing.

I've tested different spacing for direct seeded vegetables over the years and have put my recommendations on the **Vegetable Spacing Guide**. Just like the transplanted vegetables, the spacing guide assumes you're planting your seeds in rows down the length of the bed.

For example, if you look at carrots on the guide, it says to plant four to five rows down the length of the bed. If you love carrots and want to fill a whole bed with them (I do!), then simply plant four rows down the length of the bed.

4 ROWS CARROTS

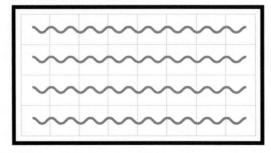

If you're not filling the whole bed with carrots, that's fine, just use the rest of the space to plant another vegetable or two.

4 ROWS CARROTS

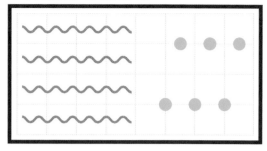

6 BROCCOLI

What does this mean for garden planning?

The **Vegetable Spacing Guide** has been calculated using a typical raised bed, which is 4 feet wide and any length. In general, garden beds should be no more than 4 feet wide because you want to be able to reach into the middle of each bed without having to step on the soil. In my garden, I have a mix of 4-foot-wide cedar raised beds and 3½-foot-wide mounded beds. I simply adjust some of the vegetable spacing to fit a narrower bed.

For example, in my raised bed I plant five rows of carrots, but in my mounded beds I plant four rows of carrots. Gardening is all about experimentation, so feel free to try out different spacing and keep track of your results.

VEGETABLE SPACING GUIDE

This spacing guide is based on a 4-foot-wide garden bed. Adjust your spacing if your garden beds are narrower or wider.

Transplanted Vegetables	
Basil	4 rows, 12" btw plants
Bok Choy	4 rows, 12" btw plants
Broccoli	2 rows, 12" btw plants
Brussels Sprouts	2 rows, 18" btw plants
Cabbage	3 rows, 18" btw plants
Cauliflower	2 rows, 18" btw plants
Celery	3 rows, 12" btw plants
Collards	2 rows, 12" btw plants
Cucumber	3 rows, 12" btw plants
Eggplant	3 rows, 18" btw plants
Fennel	4 rows, 12" btw plants
Garlic	6" btw all plants
Kale	3 rows, 12" btw plants
Leeks	6" btw all plants
Lettuce	5 rows, 12" btw plants
Melon	1 row, 18" btw plants
Onions	6" btw all plants
Parsley	3 rows, 12" btw plants
Peppers	3 rows, 18" btw plants
Potatoes	2 rows, 12" btw plants
Pumpkin	1 row, 18" btw plants
Shallots	6" btw all plants
Squash, Summer	1 row, 12" btw plants
Squash, Winter	1 row, 18" btw plants

Transplanted Vegetables Cont'd	
Sweet Potatoes	2 rows, 12" btw plants
Tomatoes	2 rows, 18" btw plants
Tomatlos	2 rows, 18" btw plants
Perennial Herbs:	You'll likely plant only one or two plants of each herb.

Direct Seeded Vegetables	
Arugula	5 rows
Beans	3 rows
Beets	4 rows
Carrots	4 rows
Cilantro	5 rows
Corn	2 rows
Dill	5 rows
Edamame	3 rows
Kohlrabi	4 rows
Okra	3 rows
Parsnip	4 rows
Peas	2 rows
Radish	5 rows
Salad Mix	6 rows
Scallions	6 rows
Spinach	4 rows
Swiss Chard	3 rows
Turnips	4 rows

Mixing Up Your Plantings for Interest

If you're a new gardener, or you like things to be straightforward and simple in your garden, then planting in rows is a great way to go. But if you like to experiment a little, or you're a creative gardener at heart (like me!), then there are a few ways you can stray from the traditional planting in rows.

Mixed Rows

Each summer I plant lots of beets and carrots for fall and early winter harvesting. Because I plant such a large amount, I usually just fill a few beds with all carrots and all beets. One year, I decided to alternate the rows in the beds—planting every other row in carrots and beets. I loved the contrast between the feathery carrot tops and the more solid beet leaves. It added just the right amount of interest to the bed instead of having it be a full bed of one vegetable.

You can do this with many different vegetables, but be careful to choose vegetables that will grow alongside one another well. Since beets and carrots both grow upright, I knew they wouldn't interfere with one another or crowd each other out.

Alternate Planting Directions

Instead of planting your rows down the length of the garden bed, consider switching the direction of the rows to go across the width of the garden bed. This creates more of a block planting pattern and provides more visual interest than just long rows down a garden bed.

For this planting pattern, try pairing vegetables with different textures next to each other. For example, in the photo on the opposite page, I planted feathery carrots to contrast with the more substantial leaves of beets and the tall, serrated leaves of cilantro. I even added in a block of flowers for a pop of color.

Again, make sure you're pairing vegetables that play well together. Don't plant anything too tall or it may shade out the vegetables around it. Plus, some vegetables like zucchini grow huge, so they're often better left in their own section of the garden.

Don't be afraid to experiment with your own ideas for spacing and planting designs. Gardening is best approached with an attitude of experimentation. Trying out different ideas and seeing what works is part of the fun.

As long as you're keeping records and notes on your garden map, you're not going to make the same mistake twice. You're in this for the long term, not just for one year, so after running different experiments over several years, you'll settle into what works best for you. And along the way, if you kill all of your lettuce because you planted it behind your tomatoes, chalk it up as a learning experience and don't feel like a failure. Next year you'll do better! Even the most experienced gardeners have things that don't work out each year.

What does this mean for garden planning?

Use the **Vegetable Spacing Guide** as simply that, a guide to optimal spacing. Print out a copy and take it with you when you go out to your garden to start planting and keep track of your spacing if you decide to experiment.

If you're mixing different plants in the same rows and beds, consider pairing vegetables that grow to the same size and have similar days to harvest.

SIMPLE RECORD-KEEPING

So you've ordered your seeds and thought a bit about how you'd like to lay things out— the final step before your seeds arrive should be setting up your record keeping system and preparing a map for your initial planting of the season.

By including a few simple steps in your gardening routine, you can stop recreating the wheel each year and build upon your successes instead. Creating a garden map and using it to keep records helps you become a better gardener over time. You train yourself to pay attention to what's happening in the garden, and that knowledge assists your learning and skill building from year to year.

Keeping Records Makes You a Better Gardener

When I first started gardening, I'd stick the little variety marker right in the soil of the garden next to the plant after I planted a seedling. Of course, by the end of the season, the tag would disappear or fade from the sun and then I wouldn't know which plant was which variety. I'd feel frustrated when there was a pepper that I loved and wanted to grow again, or a tomato that didn't produce well that I would rather not grow next year, but I'd have no idea what they were because the tag was gone.

One day while working in my garden, I was struck by a genius idea: "I should make a map of my garden!" I exclaimed to myself. I ran back to my house, grabbed a piece of paper from the printer and a pencil, and then stood at the entrance to my garden and sketched a quick map of the garden beds.

Then, I went over the lines with a sharpie marker, made a copy, and wrote the current year on the top of the map. After that, each time I planted something in my garden I wrote down the date, variety, and how much I planted. I didn't have to worry about the tags disappearing or losing track of what I planted ever again!

After several years of keeping simple records, I realized that I was reducing the amount of guesswork that went into my garden each season. My records began to show me the way to a more efficient and productive garden. I learned important things like 220 garlic plants were the perfect amount to provide us with plenty to use throughout the winter, eight basil plants made all the pesto I needed for the year, and seven kale plants allowed me to make as many massaged kale salads as my heart desired.

I didn't have to guess anymore about how many plants I might need each season. I simply consulted my records and made an educated decision. I trimmed the fat from my garden and I stopped wasting time and money planting things I didn't use, didn't like, or that didn't perform well.

I also started to hone in on the best time to plant different vegetables. Because I've kept track of the date when I plant my fall spinach each year, I know the sweet spot for planting is the third week in August. That's the planting time that does the best from year to year.

Having a garden map and keeping simple records helps you become a better gardener over time. You train yourself to pay attention to what's happening in the garden and that knowledge assists your learning and skill building from year to year.

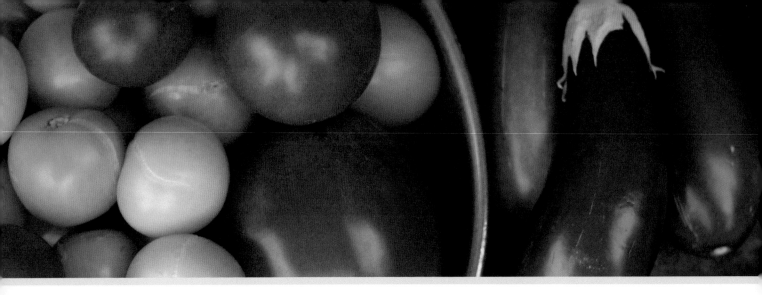

How to Create Your Garden Map

The good news is that making your map can be as simple or as involved as you'd like. When I drew my first garden map, I stood outside my garden and drew a quick outline of each of the beds. The map was more like a rough sketch of my garden space than a precisely drawn map. It worked perfectly fine for seven years.

At my current house, I brought out the measuring tape and drew the garden to scale. I measured the width and length of each bed and the space between the paths and laid it all out on graph paper.

These are the two options for making a map of your garden—the bare-bones approach and the advanced approach. The bare bones approach is to simply sketch your garden on paper without worrying about the measurements. You're basically drawing the garden beds freehand on a piece of paper so you can write down what you plant in each one throughout the season.

The advanced approach is to create a scale drawing of your garden by using a measuring tape and drawing it out on graph paper. The main reason to create an exact drawing is if you want to plan out what you're going to plant in every garden bed on paper before the season starts as we talked about in the previous section. Because you have the measurements of the garden beds, you can calculate exactly how many plants or feet of each vegetable you'll be able to fit in each one. (See **Tips for Planning Out Your Garden on Paper** on page 114.)

For most gardeners, the bare bones map is the best choice. I encourage you to choose this option unless you're a very experienced gardener.

Ultimately, whatever map-making method you choose doesn't really matter—just get the map done!

When your map is drawn, go over the lines in a darker marker or pen. This will be your master copy. Keep your master copy on file so you can change it if needed. Make a handful of Xerox copies or scan the master copy into your computer and print it out. At the beginning of each season, pull out a fresh copy of the map and start recording.

Get in the habit of taking your map out with you when you're planting in the garden. Keep it simple and record the date of planting, vegetable, variety, and how many you planted. Keep all of your notes on this map and you'll start to have a blueprint for your garden that will keep you from reinventing the wheel each season.

And if you're not sure where you should keep your map, start a garden binder! It's the easiest way to keep all of your gardening information in an easily accessible place. We talk more about creating a garden binder on pg. 118.

Dig In:

Gather your supplies and take a trip out to your garden to draw your garden map Remember, it's better to create a simple map than nothing at all!

SMART TIP

The two most important things you need to record on your garden map are what variety you planted and the date you planted it.

These two bits of information are extremely valuable. Over time they'll help you repeat your successes, like continuing to grow your favorite varieties, and tweak the things that didn't go so well, like planting your lettuce too late in the season.

BONUS VIDEO: I give you an up close and personal tour of my recordkeeping and garden binder in a short video at creativevegetablegardener.com/smart-planning-book

Tips for Planning Your Garden on Paper

A few years ago, I managed a quarter acre youth farm as part of an educational program. Each winter, I planned the entire garden on paper. I measured the planting beds on the farm and created a scale map on graph paper. I plotted out how many of each vegetable would be planted in each garden bed, calculated how many seeds I needed to order, and then how many seedlings we'd need to start in the greenhouse.

This was a lot of work and it made my brain hurt! But it felt like a necessary task when running a large garden and educational program that involved a huge number of people.

If you feel a sense of dread when thinking about planning your garden to this detail, I have good news for you: **you don't have to do it**! (And here's a little secret between you and me—I don't plan my home garden this way, ever.)

A lot of gardeners ask me whether they should decide exactly where in their garden they're going to plant every vegetable before the season starts. And my response? *"Not if you don't want to."* If planning your entire garden sounds like an unpleasant chore to you, then don't do it. In my gardening universe, it's okay, and maybe even preferable, to wing it with that part of the garden.

You can decide what vegetables you're growing, order your seeds, start or buy your plants, and then just decide where you're going to put everything in spring when you get out into your garden. That's basically what I do.

But there's a catch. You still need to have a garden map and keep track of what you plant and when throughout the season, even if you're winging it.

If the task of planning out your entire garden sounds like fun, then go for it. It's definitely an advanced gardening topic, but here are some tips to get you started.

STEP 1: You'll need a scale map of your garden like we discussed in the previous section. When you make copies of your map darken the resolution so the graph lines show up in the copies.

TIP: If you have a big garden it may be hard to keep notes on a small map.
I took the master copy of my map to the copy store and blew it up to a larger size that still fits in my binder. It contains a lot more space to write now!

STEP 2: Start filling in what you're going to plant in each garden bed. If you're not sure of the spacing between vegetables, consult the **Vegetable Spacing Guide** on page 103.

For example, if you want to plant six broccoli plants in spring, the **Vegetable Spacing Guide** lists the optimal spacing as 12" between plants, two rows to a (4-foot-wide) garden bed. (See illustration below.) Use the grid lines to draw in one plant every 12" on one of your garden beds.

TIP: All vegetable seedlings should be planted in a staggered, or triangular, pattern like the illustrations on this page. This allows them more room to grow and compete less with neighboring plants for space and nutrients.

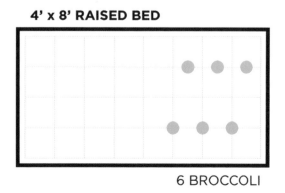

4' x 8' RAISED BED

6 BROCCOLI

STEP 3: Continue this process for each vegetable you want to plant, filling in the rows or plants in each garden bed.

For example, if you want to plant carrots in the remainder of the broccoli bed, the **Vegetable Spacing Guide** lists the spacing as 3-4 rows down the length of the bed. Fill in the carrot rows on the map.

4 ROWS CARROTS

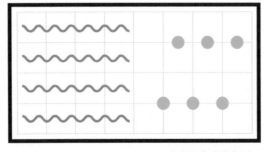

6 BROCCOLI

STEP 4: Continue filling in the rest of your garden beds with the vegetables you'd like to plant. Then, insert the dates when you'll be planting each vegetable. Use the **Create Your Own Spring Planting Schedule** worksheet to figure out your planting timeline.

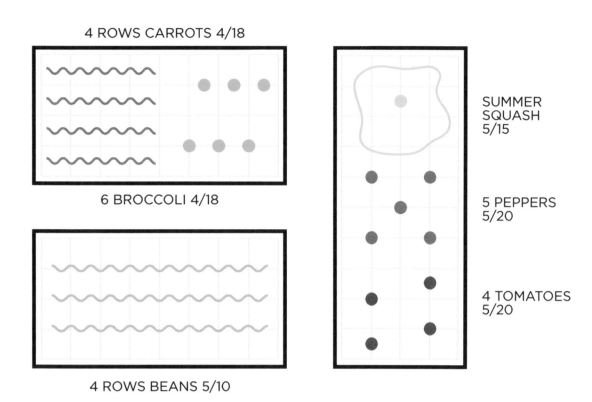

4 ROWS CARROTS 4/18

6 BROCCOLI 4/18

4 ROWS BEANS 5/10

SUMMER SQUASH 5/15

5 PEPPERS 5/20

4 TOMATOES 5/20

STEP 5: Once you have your garden mapped out, you'll be able to work backwards to figure out how many seeds you'll need to order and how many seedlings you'll need to buy or start at home if you haven't done that already.

STEP 6: Things don't always go as planned when you get into the garden in spring, so make sure you have another blank map to write down what actually happened.

This planning technique is an advanced gardening skill. It's very similar to the process vegetable farmers use in the winter to plan out their whole season. It's definitely not necessary, so again, don't do it if you don't want to!

Create Your Garden Binder

Now that you've got your plan all figured out out you'll need a place to keep it safe. Where should that be? How about a garden binder! Many years ago, when I started keeping better records of my garden, I wanted to keep everything in an easily accessible place.

After thinking about various solutions for a while, I had the great idea to start a garden binder. I dug out an old binder from my home office, grabbed my newly drawn garden map and planting schedule, punched a few holes in them, and inserted them into the binder. That was many years ago and I've used my garden binder ever since!

Over the years I've trained myself to take my binder out to the garden with me when planting so I can keep track of exactly what I'm doing. Every time I plant a vegetable I write down the date, variety and amount planted.

My binder is also where I keep my planting schedule, handouts from classes and workshops I attend, and a blank page for notes I want to jot down about the current season. My binder has become an essential part of my gardening routine and has helped me become a more observant, and thus better, gardener over time.

Dig In:

Your assignment is to start your own garden binder today! The first things to put in there are your garden map and your spring planting schedule. Feel free to print out any of the other worksheets from this book and add them as well. Don't forget to include a blank page where you can write down thoughts and ideas for the future.

The love of
gardening is a
seed once sown
that never dies.

— Gertrude Jekyll

Closing

You did it! You took an important step towards being a more successful and smarter gardener—planning your garden before the season begins. Simple garden planning will set you up for a season where you'll get more of what you really want from your garden: food, beauty, and joy. And hopefully a little less of what you don't want: stress and failure.

Now that you've planned your garden once, it will go much more easily and quickly next year. You've created a template that you'll be able to use over again each season. And because you'll be keeping records and taking notes, you'll tweak and shape the process to fit your own personal garden and lifestyle.

That's what is so exciting about this planning process. I've shown you the template, but now you can take it and run with it!

The subject of this book is garden planning, but the underlying intent is to help you love gardening in a way that brings a deeper joy and richness to your life. I believe that when you have a successful garden, whatever success means to you, then gardening is more fun. And when gardening is more fun, you're more likely to become a lifelong gardener—someone who can't imagine her life without a garden in it.

Growing your own food is a radical act. In a world where our hands spend more time than ever working with computers, there's an elemental pleasure in creating something with our own two hands. When we can walk into a grocery store and buy any fruit or vegetable we want at any time of the season, eating fresh food straight from our gardens can be a life-changing experience.

Having a garden is casting your vote for a future where people enjoy (and demand) real food, pursue a connection with nature, and seek the satisfaction of creating something with their own hands.

Together we're building a community of gardening addicts who are passionate about learning new ways to live healthy and fulfilling lives. This is important work, and know that I'm here to support you. I genuinely care about your ongoing success and improvement as a gardener. We're in this together!

Happy Gardening!

Megan

About the Author

As an urban girl growing up in one of the largest cities in the US, I never touched a vegetable plant until the summer I turned 26. That's when I moved from my big-city life in San Francisco to a rural farm town of 100 people in Northeastern Missouri. After I got over the shock to my system, I fell in love with gardening and the rest, as they say, is history!

I've spent the last 15 years of my life teaching hundreds of people of all ages how to get their hands dirty growing food in Madison, WI. I developed one of the early kids' gardening programs in Madison and a half-acre youth farm. I've started my own home garden from a sad scrap of dirt and created an urban gardening class series that often has waiting lists. Through my business, The Creative Vegetable Gardener, I encourage and educate gardeners how to successfully grow their own food and get the most from their vegetable gardens. My secret mission is to create a legion of gardening addicts.

KEEP IN TOUCH

Connect with other likeminded gardeners from around the world in my free Facebook group, Creative Gardener Challenges. You can request to join our group at this link: https://www.facebook.com/groups/MakeYourHarvestLast/

Receive my best gardening advice for free, in the season you need it most, when you sign up for my email list at creativevegetablegardener.com

Happy Gardening!

Megan

VEGGIE ESSENTIALS CHEAT SHEET

Veggie	Harvest Season	How much food will I harvest?	How big do the plants grow?	How many days until I get a harvest
Arugula	Spring Fall	Short Harvest 1-2 cuttings/week	Small	Short, 21-40 days
Asparagus	Spring	Short Harvest 1+ lb. per plant	Medium, Grows in clusters of spears	Long, 3-4 years to start harvesting
Beans, Fresh	Summer Fall	Short Harvest (Bush) 2-3 weeks of harvest per planting Long Harvest (Pole) Many weeks of harvest as plant puts on new growth	Medium (Bush) Large (Pole)	Medium, 50-65 days
Beans, Dry	Summer Fall	Short Harvest Small handful per plant	Medium (Bush) Large (Pole)	Long, 90-105 days
Beets	Spring Summer Fall Winter	Plant One— Harvest One	Medium	Medium, 45-60 days
Bok Choy	Spring Fall	Plant One— Harvest One	Medium	Medium, 45-60 days
Broccoli	Spring Fall	Plant One— Harvest One	Medium	Medium, 50-75 days
Brussels Sprouts	Fall Winter	Short Harvest 1+ lbs per plant	Large, Tall	Long, 90-110 days
Cabbage	Spring Summer Fall	Plant One— Harvest One	Large, Wide	Medium, 65-105 days
Carrots	Summer Fall Winter	Plant One— Harvest One	Medium	Medium, 50-80 days
Cauliflower	Spring Fall	Plant One— Harvest One	Medium	Medium, 50-80 days
Celery	Summer Fall	Plant One—Harvest One/ Long Harvest 1 bunch per plant	Medium	Long, 85 days

Direct Seed or Transplant	Favorite Varieties*	Garden Planning Notes
DS	Astro	Planted in early spring and again for fall. Bolts in hot weather. Often grows better in fall due to the cooler weather.
T	Jersey Knight	Buy crowns from a seed catalog or local nursery. Perennial that takes 3-4 years to establish. Lives up to 25 years.
DS	Maxibel Dragon Tongue Trilogy	Kids love Dragon Tongue beans! Trilogy is a mix of green, purple and yellow beans.
DS	Cherokee Trail of Tears Vermont Cranberry	Dry beans need to be left on the plant until they're completely dry; this is often at the end of the season.
DS	Red Ace Early Wonder Tall Top	Try growing Touchstone Gold and Chioggia varieties.
DS or T	Joy Choi	Great for a quick spring crop. Grow as baby greens or a full head.
T	Spring: Gypsy Fall: Arcadia, Marathon	There are different varieties for spring, summer and fall plantings. Read the descriptions.
T	Gustus Nautic Diablo	Can be challenging if you don't grow the right variety for your garden. Keep experimenting!
T	Ruby Perfection Tendersweet	Grow a mix of purple and green cabbages.
DS	Bolero Yellow Sun Deep Purple	Mix yellow, purple, and orange seeds together in one bed to get a fun mix of colors.
T	Bishop	Can be difficult to grow. Success is very variety dependent.
T	Tango	Can be tougher than grocery store celery. Freeze for winter soups. You can harvest the whole bunch at once, or pick stalks individually.

Veggie	Harvest Season	How much food will I harvest?	How big do the plants grow?	How many days until I get a harvest
KAD - KAPYSTA **Collards** *KALE*	Spring Summer Fall Winter	Long Harvest 1 harvest/week	Medium/ Large	Medium, 50-60 days
Corn	Summer Fall	Short Harvest Less than 10 per stalk	Large, Tall	Medium, 65-85 days
Cucumbers	Summer Fall	Long Harvest 2+ fruits/week	Large, Sprawling vine	Medium, 50-65 days
Edamame (Soybeans)	Summer Fall	Short Harvest 20-30+ pods per plant	Medium	Long, 75-90 days
BAKLAŽÁN **Eggplant**	Summer Fall	Long Harvest 8-15 per plant	Medium	Medium, 55-75 days
FENYKL **Fennel**	Spring	Plant One— Harvest One	Medium	Medium, 50-85 days
Garlic	Summer	Plant One— Harvest One	Medium	Long, 7-8 months
Kale	Spring Summer Fall Winter	Long Harvest Several bunches/ month	Medium	Medium, 50-65 days
KEDLUBNA **Kohlrabi**	Spring Fall	Plant One— Harvest One	Medium	Medium, 37-80 days
PÓR **Leeks**	Fall Winter	Plant One— Harvest One	Medium	Long, 75-120 days
Lettuce, Head	Spring Fall	Plant One— Harvest One	Small/ Medium, depends on variety	Short, 30-60 days
Lettuce, Salad Mix	Spring Fall	Short Harvest 2-4 cuttings per planting	Small	Short, 25-40 days
Melons	Summer Fall	Short Harvest 2-10 per plant	Large, Sprawling vine	Long, 70-120 days

Direct Seed or Transplant	Favorite Varieties*	Garden Planning Notes
T	Vates	Gets sweeter and more tasty with the cooler temperatures of fall.
DS	Silver Queen Glass Gem Dakota Black	Needs to be planted in a large block for pollination, at least 4 rows wide. Growing popcorn is fun with kids.
DS or T	Diva Northern Pickling Lemon	Great for a trellis because they have tendrils that let them climb naturally.
DS	Tohya Envy	Difficult to find at the farmers' market and often expensive. Can be frozen for winter eating
T	Dancer Pingtung Long Rosa Bianca	Dancer is my all-time favorite eggplant. Very productive and a beautiful electric purple color.
DS	Preludio Bronze	Plant early. Doesn't like hot weather.
DS	Porcelain Types Music	Planted in late fall and harvested in July of the following season. Buy seed from a farmer or catalog, or save your own. Porcelain types are best for storage.
T	Scarlet Toscano Redbor	Also, Red Russian, Winterbor, and Dwarf Blue Curled.
DS or T	Winner Kolibri	Plant both purple and white varieties for a mix.
T	King Richard Lancelot Lincoln	Last a long time in the fridge after harvest in late fall. Or make potato leek soup to freeze.
DS or T	Butterhead Magenta Nevada Red Salad Bowl	Transplant seedlings to get exact spacing. Mix red and green varieties in the same bed. There are many amazing varieties of lettuce.
DS	Encore Mix Mesclun Mix	Cut and come again crop. Harvest with scissors and let re-grow to harvest again.
DS or T	Sun Jewel Sarah's Choice	Melons are difficult to grow in northern climates. Most farmers who do it successfully use black plastic over their beds.

Veggie	Harvest Season	How much food will I harvest?	How big do the plants grow?	How many days until I get a harvest
Okra	Summer Fall	Long Harvest 5-10 week per plant	Large, Tall	Medium, 50-60 days
Onions	Summer	Plant One— Harvest One	Small	Long, 90-110 days
Parsnips	Fall Winter	Plant One— Harvest One	Medium	Long, 110-120 days
Peas	Spring	Short Harvest 50+ per plant	Large, Tall vine	Medium, 50-65 days
Peppers, Sweet	Summer Fall	Long Harvest 3-10+ per plant	Medium	Medium, 70-85 days
Peppers, Hot	Summer Fall	Long Harvest 10-50+ per plant	Medium	Med/Long 60-100 days
Potatoes	Summer Fall	Short Harvest 5-10 per plant	Medium	Med/Long, 70-120 days
Pumpkins	Fall	Short Harvest 2-10 per plant	Large, Sprawling vine	Long, 85-120 days
Radishes	Spring Fall	Plant One— Harvest One	Small	Short, 21-30 days
Raspberries	Summer Fall	Short Harvest Up to 20+ berries per cane	Large, Tall	Perennial
Rhubarb	Spring	Short Harvest Several lbs./month	Large, Wide	Perennial
Scallions	Spring Summer Fall Winter	Plant One— Harvest One	Small	Medium, 65-70 days

Direct Seed or Transplant	Favorite Varieties*	Garden Planning Notes
DS or T	Clemson Spineless Red Burgundy	Grows tall like corn. Relative of hibiscus with beautiful flowers. Can be grown successfully in northern climates.
T	Red Wing Pontiac Patterson	Also, Ailsa Craig and Cortland. If you want to store your onions grow storage varieties. If not, grow varieties for fresh eating.
DS	Lancer	Can overwinter in many northern climates and be dug up in spring.
DS	Sugar Ann Golden Sweet	Best grown on a trellis. There are different varieties of peas—shell, snow and sweet.
T	Carmen Jimmy Nardello Lively Yellow	Also, Biscayne, Escamillo. If you've had trouble growing red peppers try Carmen—you won't be disappointed!
T	Jalapeno Fish Santa Fe Grande	Hot pepper plants tend to produce a lot of peppers. Plant sparingly unless you love them!
DS	Red Norland Purple Viking Purple Varieties	Buy seed potatoes from a seed catalog or nursery. Try a purple fleshed variety if you have kids.
DS or T	Cargo Snowball	Take up lots of room. Fun to grow with kids.
DS	Cherriette Easter Egg Beauty Heart	Great for a quick spring crop. Beauty Heart is a radish like no other!
T	Caroline Polana	Takes a few years to establish. Buy canes from a local nursery or thin out a friend's patch. Grow summer and fall bearing varieties for a longer harvest.
T	Any	Takes a year or two to establish. Easy to grow from a piece of root from a friend's plant.
DS or T	White Spear Evergreen Hardy White Deep Purple	Plant every few weeks for a continued harvest all season. Can survive the winter in cold climates and will start re-growing in spring.

Veggie	Harvest Season	How much food will I harvest?	How big do the plants grow?	How many days until I get a harvest
Shallots	Summer Fall	Plant One— Harvest One	Small	Long, 110 days
Spinach	Spring Fall Winter	Short Harvest (Spring)/ Long Harvest (Fall/Winter) 2-5+ cuttings per planting	Small	Short, 25-40 days
Squash, Summer	Summer Fall	Long Harvest 3+/week per plant	Large, Wide	Medium, 45-60 days
Squash, Winter	Fall	Short Harvest 3-10 per plant	Large, Sprawling vine	Long, 85-120 days
Strawberries	Summer	Short Harvest 10-20+ per plant	Small, Can spread	Perennial
Sweet Potatoes	Fall	Short Harvest 5-10 per plant	Large, Sprawling vine	Long, 90-100 days
Swiss Chard	Spring Summer Fall	Long Harvest Several bunches/month	Medium	Medium, 50-60 days
Tomatillos	Summer Fall	Long Harvest 50-100+ per plant	Large, Tall	Medium, 60-70 days
Tomatoes, Cherry	Summer Fall	Long Harvest Hundreds per plant	Large, Tall	Medium, 55-60 days
Tomatoes, Roma	Summer Fall	Long Harvest 20-50+ per plant	Large, Tall	Medium, 60-85 days
Tomatoes, Slicing	Summer Fall	Long Harvest 20-50+ per plant	Large, Tall	Medium, 60-85 days
Turnips	Spring Fall Winter	Plant One— Harvest One	Medium	Short, 30-50 days
Other:				
Other:				

(handwritten notes: "MEX. RAJČE" above Tomatillos, "FIALOVÉ" below Tomatillos, "TUŘÍN, VODNICE" above Turnips)

Direct Seed or Transplant	Favorite Varieties*	Garden Planning Notes
T	Camelot Conservor	Grow more like garlic than onions, forming a cluster of bulbs. Plant early.
DS	Giant Winter Corvair	Can be a short harvest in spring because it doesn't like hot weather. Fall planted spinach can be a longer harvest. Survives the winter in very cold climates.
DS or T	Raven Zephyr Sunburst	Start a few summer squash seed indoors if you want a jump on the season. Each plant produces a lot of fruit. A lot!
DS or T	Waltham Delicata Table Queen	Lots of interesting varieties. Butternut can store for many months of winter in a cool basement.
T	Earliglow Jewel	Perennial plant, takes a year to establish. Buy plants from a seed catalog or local nursery.
T	Beauregard	Buy slips (vines) from a seed catalog or local nursery.
DS or T	Ruby Red Bright Lights	Beautiful, edible ornamental with electric colors.
T	Toma Verde Purple	Need at least two plants for pollination.
T	Sun Gold Super Sweet 100	Sun Gold is the best variety out there!
T	Amish Paste Viva Italia San Marzano	Amish paste is my favorite for making sauce.
T	Moonglow Green Zebra Yellow Perfection	My three favorite tomatoes for fresh eating.
DS	Hakurei	Best variety! If you don't think you like turnips, try these. Quick spring or fall crop.

HERBS

Herb	Harvest Season	How much food will I harvest?	How big do the plants grow?	How many days until I get a harvest
Basil	Summer Fall	Long Harvest Several cuttings/month per plant	Small/ Medium	Medium, 60-85 days
Cilantro	Spring Fall	Short Harvest (Spring)/ Long Harvest (Fall/Winter) 2-5 cuttings per planting	Small	Medium, 50-60 days
Dill	Summer Fall	Short Harvest 3-5 flower heads per plant	Large, Tall	Medium/ Long 40 (leaf) - 105 (seed)
Garlic Chives	Spring Summer Fall Winter	Long Harvest 1+ bundle/week	Small, Can spread	Perennial
Marjoram	Spring Summer Fall Winter	Long Harvest 1+ bundle/week	Small, Can spread	Perennial
Mint	Spring Summer Fall Winter	Long Harvest 1+ bundle/week	Small, Very invasive	Perennial
Onion Chives	Spring Summer Fall	Long Harvest 1+ bundle/week	Medium, Can spread	Perennial
Oregano	Spring Summer Fall	Long Harvest 1+ bundle/week	Small, Can spread	Perennial
Parsley	Spring Summer Fall	Long Harvest 1+ bundle/week	Medium	Medium, 75 days
Rosemary	Summer Fall	Long Harvest 1+ bundle/week	Medium/ Large in mild climates	Perennial
Sage	Spring Summer Fall Winter	Long Harvest 1+ bundle/week	Medium/ Large, Depending on variety	Perennial

Direct Seed or Transplant	Favorite Varieties*	Garden Planning Notes
T	Genovese Eleonora Purple Ruffles	Annual herb, must be replanted each year.
DS	Santo Calypso	Annual herb. Will go to seed in hot weather. Great for fall planting. Keep in part shade and it will last longer.
DS	Bouquet Fernleaf	Annual herb, must be replanted each year. Re-seeds itself prolifically .
T	Any	Perennial herb. Difficult to start from seed, best to buy a seedling.
T	Sweet	Perennial herb. Difficult to start from seed, best to buy a seedling
T	Peppermint Spearmint Chocolate Mint	Mint is highly invasive! It can take over your entire garden. Grow it in a container, or submerge it in a pot into the soil to control the spread.
T	Any	Perennial herb. Difficult to start from seed, best to buy a seedling.
T	Golden Greek	Perennial herb. Difficult to start from seed, best to buy a seedling.
T	Italian Flat Leaf	Annual herb. Difficult to start from seed, best to buy a seedling. There are curly and flat leaf varieties.
T	Gorizia	Perennial herb. Difficult to start from seed, best to buy a seedling. Needs to come inside for winter in cold areas.
T	Golden Tricolor	Perennial herb. Difficult to start from seed, best to buy a seedling. Lots of colorful varieties.

Herb	Harvest Season	How much food will I harvest?	How big do the plants grow?	How many days until I get a harvest
Tarragon	Spring Summer Fall Winter	Long Harvest 1+ bundle/week	Large, Tall, spreading	Perennial
Thyme	Spring Summer Fall Winter	Long Harvest 1+ bundle/week	Small, Can spread	Perennial

*Most of these varieties can be ordered through Johnny's Selected Seeds, High Mowing Seeds, or Seed Savers Exchange

SIZE KEY:
Small = 6-12 inches
Medium = 2-3 ft.
Large = over 3 ft.

NOTES

Direct Seed or Transplant	Favorite Varieties*	Garden Planning Notes
T	French	Perennial herb. Difficult to start from seed, best to buy a seedling.
T	Silver-edged Lemon	Perennial herb. Difficult to start from seed, best to buy a seedling. Lots of neat varieties!

NOTES

MISTAKES TO AVOID:

1. NO PERMANENT BEDS + PATHS (STOP TILLING!)

2. GROWING THINGS YOU DON'T EAT

3. WASTING MONEY / OBS. ON LINE
   PORÁDNĚ ROZMYSLET, CO KOUPIT

4. GROWING GRASS IN THE GARDEN
   (jů flat a za mim mechnný fídrníky prozítti...)

5. OVERWATERING YOUR GARDEN
   1 INCH OF WATER PER WEEK
   (GERMINATTE EVERY 1-2 DAYS)
   A RAIN GAUGE # HOW MUCH WATER IF IT RAINS

Printed in Great Britain
by Amazon